PALLET WOOD PROJECTS
FOR OUTDOOR SPACES

PALLET WOOD PROJECTS FOR OUTDOOR SPACES

35 CONTEMPORARY PROJECTS FOR GARDEN FURNITURE & ACCESSORIES

Hester van Overbeek

CICO BOOKS

LONDON NEW YORK

DEDICATION

Sweet little Kiki, may your appearance in this book make you to want to build too!

Published in 2019 by CICO Books
An imprint of Ryland Peters & Small Ltd
20–21 Jockey's Fields
London WC1R 4BW
341 E 116th St
New York, NY 10029

www.rylandpeters.com

10 9 8 7 6 5 4 3

Text © Hester van Overbeek 2019
Design, illustration, and photography
© CICO Books 2019

A CIP catalog record for this book is available from the Library of Congress and the British Library.

ISBN: 978 1 78249 715 8

Printed in China

Editor: Gillian Haslam
Designer: Geoff Borin
Photographer: James Gardiner
Stylist: Hester van Overbeek

Editors: Anna Galkina and Pete Jorgensen
Publishing assistant: Gurjant Mandair
In-house designer: Eliana Holder
Art director: Sally Powell
Production controller: David Hearn
Publishing manager: Penny Craig
Publisher: Cindy Richards

CONTENTS

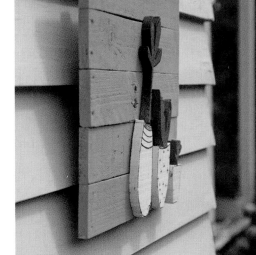

INTRODUCTION

I love being outside, and as soon as the sun is out you can find me in the garden. Actually the sun doesn't even have to be shining—as long as it doesn't rain, I'm there! I love to relax outside and use my small garden as a place for entertaining, with friends frequently calling in for brunch, coffee and cake, or a summer barbecue. For this reason, I like my deck to look like an extension of my living room, filled with practical and decorative items built from wood. And which type of wood has a great patina, is beautifully worn, and no two pieces look the same? Pallet wood, of course!

Pallets have become a hot upcycling material in recent years and just a quick browse on the Internet will show you hundreds of ways of turning a pallet into a piece of furniture. Raise your hands if you have been to a bar or store where the furniture is made out of pallets?

However, I see the pallet as more than just a building block. I like taking pallets apart and reusing the wood in a completely different way. The humble pallet is a great budget-friendly raw material, and the possibilities for using its wooden planks are endless! However, in case you don't fancy taking yours apart or you are looking for a quick build, I have included a few projects where I kept the pallet intact (see the Mosaic Inlay Table on page 28, the Pallet Sofas on page 49, and the Easy Pallet Planter on page 87).

I hope you have fun building your favorite projects from this book. There are easy, decorative builds like the Vase Rack on page 118 and the Whitewashed Lantern on page 123. There are projects that will make good use of your offcuts, like the Candle and Tealight Holders on page 114 and the Plant Stands on page 104, and there are the bigger builds like the Garden Chair on page 25 and the Chevron Table on page 46. Use my tutorials as you would use a recipe, adapting the dimensions of the project to fit the pallet wood you have available as the length and width of the planks can vary. I would love to see what you build, so please share your makes on social media and tag or mention me (find my social media handles at the back of the book).

I find it hard to believe that this is my fifth book! And as always, my little dog Kermit makes an appearance (he has snuck into a photo in all of my other books). You can find him in two of the projects here, but there is also somebody else making her first appearance—my daughter Kiki (she was just five months old when we took her photo in the play tent). Kermit is a bit of a poser, but I think he is now getting some competition from little Kiki!

Happy building!
x Hester

USING PALLET WOOD

Pallets have become the upcycling staple in recent years as they can provide a free or inexpensive source of wood and can be used in so many ways. Made from many different kinds of wood, you will never find two identical pallets.

There are standard sizes in pallets, but these can vary from one country to another—for instance, UK-sized ones are 1200 x 1000mm, while GMA (the US Grocery Manufacturers Association) ones are 48 x 40 inches. However, the ones I used for this book were all different in shape as pallets are made the world over to different sizes and standards. Just make sure the pallet you want to use hasn't been treated with chemicals (see Pallet Safety on page 10) and remove all nails and tags before handling.

WHERE TO FIND PALLETS

I source my pallets from all sorts of places—here are a few ideas to get you started.

Building yards, garden centers, and small businesses often have leftover pallets which they will let you collect for free or buy for a very reasonable price. I often ask my local timber merchant if he can add a few pallets to my wood order. Be aware that some businesses reuse the pallets and are not allowed to sell them on or give them to you, but most wood or construction companies have stacks of them and are happy to let you have some.

Construction sites are also good places to enquire about pallets. They often have their building supplies delivered on them, so ask the site manager politely and they might give you some.

Local Facebook groups are great—I have sometimes put a message up on the board and within a few hours have been offered several pallets I can pick up for free. The same applies to websites like Gumtree and Freecyle.

You can always find pallets for sale on eBay for very low prices, and sometimes they even deliver them for you.

If you love the look of pallet-wood furniture but don't want the hassle of dealing with big, heavy pallets, there are companies that source the pallet for you, take it apart, and even sand it! I use The Little Lodge (www.thelittlelodge.co.uk) here in the UK, but have a look on Google or eBay to find a pallet-wood supplier in your area.

PREPARING PALLETS

Pallet wood has been treated for outdoor use, which makes it ideal for the projects in this book. Pallets have often been transported on trucks, used on construction sites or in building yards, and left out in the open. The pallets can therefore be a little bashed or quite grubby when you acquire them, so they will need cleaning before you transform the wood into one of the following projects. I prefer cleaning the wood after I have taken the pallet apart.

First check for woodworm by looking for little holes in the pallet wood. If the wood feels lighter than you would expect, it probably has/had bugs that ate away the inside of the wood. It's difficult to know if the insects are still active, so to be safe I would discard this wood. You don't want to bring woodworm into your house or to spend time building something with wood that will not last or be strong. You can treat wood with a woodworm killer—you will find liquid treatments at your DIY store. Follow the instructions on the packet carefully, and always wear gloves, safety goggles, and a mask when using chemicals.

Also check your pallets for mold. Give the wood a sniff as sometimes you don't see mold but you can smell it. Never use moldy pieces of wood in your projects.

Always wear work gloves when handling pallet wood or other reclaimed wood, safety glasses when pulling out nails, and a dust mask when cleaning dirt off wood.

TAKING A PALLET APART

You can take a pallet apart with a crowbar and a bit of force. Wear safety googles and work gloves to protect yourself.

First look for any areas on the pallet where the wood seems slightly loose—this is the place to start. Wedge a crowbar between the layers of wood, then move the crowbar back to lift the piece of wood and loosen it. Don't try to lift the slat all the way up at this stage. Repeat at the other end of the slat, then move to the middle and do the same until the slat is ready to be lifted. Take care with the nails as they may be rusty, and make sure to remove all the tags, nails, screws, or other sharp bits using a claw hammer and pincers before handling the slat pieces further. Old hardware is probably rusty and a cut from a rusty nail or screw needs tetanus treatment, so be careful. Watch out for splinters, too.

If your project only needs short pieces of wood, you could saw the planks away from the supporting framework, saving yourself a lot of time and effort.

CLEANING PALLETS

If the pallet has been stored inside, brush off any dust and, if necessary, clean the wood with soapy water. I use dishwashing liquid and a sponge to scrub it clean, but only do this if it really needs it as you don't want to get the wood wet for no reason. Let the wood dry outside, ideally in the sun as this will speed up the process.

If the wood has been stored outside in wet conditions, you need to take a rougher approach to remove mud and debris. If you have a pressure washer, just line the wood up and spray on all sides until clean. If you don't have a pressure washer, you will need to use a bit more elbow grease. Make a cleaning solution of dishwashing liquid and bleach (see below) or borax substitute (see page 10) and scrub the wood using a steel brush. Pay particular attention to grooves and notches in the wood as you need to clean these areas more aggressively. I also use a steel wire attachment on my drill for any really hard-to-clean spots.

There are several ways to clean wood (always do this outside).

BLEACH—this produces harsh fumes so make sure the area is well ventilated before you begin (open all windows and doors to improve air circulation or ideally work outside). You should also wear gloves to protect your hands. Make a solution of 1 part bleach and 10 parts water. Apply with a sponge or scrubbing brush. You don't need to rinse the wood unless you intend to use it for food or have it around small children and pets. Let the wood dry outside, ideally in the sun.

BORAX SUBSTITUTE—this is a white mineral powder, commonly used as a natural household cleaner. Mix it with water to kill and remove mold. Mix 1 cup of borax substitute per 1 gallon (4.5 liters) of lukewarm water. Make sure to wear gloves as borax substitute may irritate your skin. Apply the solution to the wood using a sponge or scrubbing brush. Let it sit for a few minutes, then scrub the wood clean using a steel brush. Wipe the wood and let it dry, ideally in the sun or in a well-ventilated room.

DISHWASHING LIQUID—mix together 5 parts water and 1 part dishwashing liquid to create a cleaning solution. Dip a scrubbing brush in the solution and rub down the entire surface of the wood, then leave it to dry in the sun.

STEAM—I've read about people cleaning pallet wood with steam cleaners and, although I haven't tried this myself, it makes sense as the steam will sanitize wood and clean off all the dirt.

Once the wood has dried, sand it in preparation for building (see page 18).

PALLET SAFETY

There are a few checks you should make to establish whether a pallet is safe to use. If in doubt, don't use it.

• Check for spills or leakages. If you see any spills (either oil or unknown substances), reject the pallet. It is safer to use only clean ones.

• Do not use colored pallets as they are often used to transport chemicals.

• Look at the stamps on the side of the pallet—there are a few things to look out for. An IPPC (International Plant Protection Convention) logo will tell you the pallet has been made of material that will not carry invasive insect species or plant disease. The pallets will have been treated under the supervision of an agency approved to do this. Pallets without an IPPC stamp might be safe to use, but you never know for sure. The other stamp shows the method of treatment. Those marked with HT (heat treatment) are good to use; some pallets may say KD (kiln dried) and these are fine to use, too. The purpose of kiln-dried lumber is to reduce the moisture content of the wood (19% or less)—it is a means of controlling warping, fungal growth, and other features.

• NEVER ever use a pallet with the MB (methyl bromide fumigation) stamp! These are not safe to use. Methyl bromide fumigation uses a strong pesticide linked to human health problems and ozone layer depletion. The EPA (Environmental Protection Agency) lists methyl bromide as highly acute toxic.

Although it has not been used since 2005, in most countries there are still old pallets in circulation, so be warned.

There are other stamps you might see:

• DB means the wood was debarked. It doesn't matter if the pallet has this stamp, but a DB stamp means the pallet is chemical-free and thus safe to use. Don't get too concerned by the absence of this stamp though, as lots of new pallets don't carry it anymore. IPPC regulations no longer require newer pallets to have this stamp, as most modern wood treatment procedures require "debarking" as a standard part of their process.

• A country code and number may appear—a pallet made in the USA will have US on it followed by the 4-digit registration number of the supplier, GB for the UK, NL for the Netherlands, etc. EPAL is the European Pallet Association logo—this is a good one as Europe doesn't allow chemical treatment of pallets. The letters EUR mean your pallet is also a European one, but dates back to an old registration system; only use these if they also have an EPAL stamp.

• Most pallets also have a date stamp, so you can find out when they were made.

The country code and date stamps are fun to look at—for this book I had pallets made all over the world. I even found a Dutch one (NL—my native country) and I hadn't come across one of those before!

CHOOSING YOUR TOOLS

A fully equipped workshop will make building a lot easier and faster, but unless you are a professional carpenter you probably just have a basic tool kit. Most of the projects in this book have been built using a basic tool kit, i.e. the average tools you probably already have (below, these are labeled "basic"). A few projects use power tools that are more specialist (these are labeled "advanced" or "specialist")—in these cases you may be able to borrow from friends or family, or use hand tools instead. I have built up my collection of tools gradually over the years and in this book I probably use a few tools that you may not have, but alternatives are always given in those cases.

SAWS

HANDSAW (basic)—I like sawing by hand, partly because I don't have a power supply in my workshop, but also because with smaller projects, I find it is easier to do it all by hand. I often think I have more precision with a handheld saw.

FRET SAW (basic/specialist)—this was the first saw I ever used when cutting out animal shapes as a child. With its U shape and very thin blade, this saw is perfect for intricate cutting work, like the motifs in the Outdoor Art project on page 112. It has a distinctive appearance due to the depth of its frame—typically between 10 and 20 inches (25 and 50cm)—which, together with the relatively short 5-inch (12.5-cm) blade, makes this tool appear somewhat out of proportion compared to most other saws. You can also use it to saw circles or shapes inside a piece of wood. I like using a wooden clamp to support my wood as it makes it very easy to move the saw around.

JIGSAW (basic)—small and handheld, this is less intimidating than other power saws. A great first saw for the beginner DIY-er, a jigsaw will make it super-easy to cut your materials, and is especially useful if you need to cut a curve. It will not cut thick materials like pallet wood, but is great for sheets of MDF and plywood. There are specific blades for different materials, even one for cutting metal.

BOTTOM LEFT My handsaw and fret saw, with its mini saw table.
BOTTOM RIGHT My mini circular saw and jigsaw.

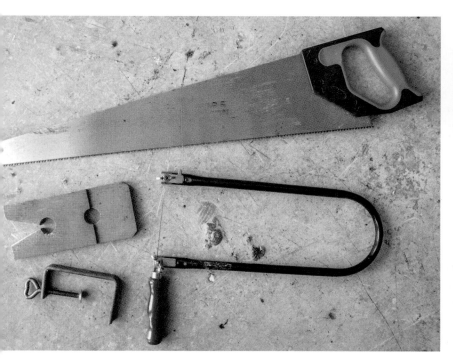

TOP LEFT AND RIGHT Miter saw.
ABOVE Reciprocating saw.

CIRCULAR SAW (advanced)—this is great if you want to add more tools to your tool box and if you need to cut thicker wood, like a door, or long lines that have to be perfectly straight (this saw only cuts straight lines). The bigger the saw blade, the thicker the wood you can cut. Most circular saws have a parallel (edge) saw guide and a laser light to help you follow your cutting line with precision. I also own a mini circular saw which can be held with one hand. When using circular saws or any kind of power tool, make sure to follow all safety instructions (see page 17).

MITER SAW (advanced)—this can make almost any cut where a specific angle is essential, which includes angled and titled cuts. You have stationary miter saws and sliding ones. A stationary miter saw has a pivoting arm which allows you to tip the blade to the side, which results in a bevel cut. I like using my sliding miter saw as it pivots but also has an arm that makes the blade slide out, so I can cut wider and thicker wood. Miter saws are great if you need to cut angles or a lot of straight cuts. Always make sure to clamp the wood you are cutting firmly in place before cutting it.

MITER BOX (basic)—the non-electric version of the miter saw, for making angled cuts using a handsaw.

RECIPROCATING SAW (advanced)—this is a power tool with a saw blade that "pushes and pulls" (reciprocates). Also known as a recip saw and Sawzall (this is a trademarked name common in the US). The saw allows you to make quick cuts through almost every material and, due to the handle, this saw is great to use on vertical surfaces like a pallet. I use mine to cut the wood away from the blocks.

SANDERS

SANDPAPER (basic)—good old sandpaper will help you out in every project. It is available in different grids, from very coarse 20 grid to very fine 600 grid paper. The finer the grid, the smoother your wood will be, but you have to build up to a super-smooth finish by sanding several times, beginning with a coarse grid and finishing with the fine grid.

Extra coarse—this is really rough paper, so only ever use it on the toughest jobs, such as removing paint.

Coarse (around the 40 grid range)—use for rough shaping and removal of paint/varnish.

Medium (grid range 60–100)—perfect all-round paper for almost any job. Use for shaping your object and final preparation for finishing.

Fine (grid 120–220)—use after a medium grid paper for smoothing raised woodgrain fibers.

Extra fine (grid up to 600)—use in between coats of paint or for polishing your projects.

PALM SANDER (basic)—for bigger sanding jobs, use a palm sander. The sanding pads (which are attached to the base of the sander using Velcro tape) are graded in the same way as sandpaper (see above). A palm sander is great for sanding large items such as furniture or projects such as the Play Tent on page 72 where you want a really smooth finish.

BELT SANDER (advanced)—useful for a very large sanding job, this is the big brother of the palm sander as it has more power and a bigger sanding surface. The sandpaper is in a continuous loop that keeps running around. Belt sanders can have a very aggressive action on wood and are normally used only for the early stages of the sanding process, or to remove material rapidly.

POWER DRIVER/DRILL

Nowadays almost all drills are cordless as they are so much easier to work with. Always have the spare battery charged so when the power runs out, you don't have to wait an hour for your drill to recharge. Always use the right drill bits for the material you are working with (buy a set of drill bits so you have a variety to use).

WOOD BITS—these have a pointed tip. Spurs on either side of the point will cut clean, straight holes. They are suitable for all types of wood and come in a huge range of sizes and lengths.

COUNTERSINK BITS—use these to make the beginning of a drill hole a bit wider so that the screw will sit flush with the wood when screwed in place.

MASONRY BITS—the shaft spirals up to a tip that is often composed of an extra-hardened material.

SPADE OR SADDLE BITS—the pointed tip begins the hole and the paddle-shaped blade bores large, wide holes. The size is clearly marked on the paddle's face.

HOLE CUTTER—a hole cutter comes in various sizes for cutting wood and metal. The drill bit cuts first, then the round cutter makes a larger hole.

HINGE CUTTER—a heavy-duty, tungsten carbide-tipped drill piece with a center point and outer spurs. Drills a 1⅜-inch (35-mm) hole the size of a cupboard door hinge. I used this for cutting a hole for the tealight holder on page 114.

Your driver/drill is used for driving in screws as well—simply insert the screwdriver into the chuck. I like using a bit holder that fits different screw bits, as this allows you to change them easily.

BELOW LEFT Different grids of sandpaper.
BELOW MIDDLE A palm sander is a must-have in your tool box.
BELOW RIGHT Selection of drill bits.

OTHER TOOLS

HAMMER—the most basic tool for fixing pieces of wood together. Available in different sizes, a standard claw hammer will be invaluable in your tool box. Use the claw at the back of the hammer to pull nails out (essential when using pallets or other old pieces of wood).

NAIL GUN—I love my nail gun as it makes building so much faster! If you do a lot of building work, I would definitely invest in a nail gun. Always follow your tool's instructions as it is a dangerous tool in unstable hands. The gun uses compressed air to push the nail into the wood, and you can adjust the depth and strength of that process. My nail gun has a built-in compressor, while the professional versions have a separate one which makes them even more powerful.

GLUE GUN—this little gadget heats up glue sticks, making a strong bond between materials, for example in the Letter Planter project on page 99.

SCREWDRIVER— choose either a flat-head (slot-head) or a Phillips (cross-head), depending on the screws you are using. I prefer a Phillips as they fit in the screw head better, so are a lot easier to use. Use a screwdriver that matches the shape and size of your screw to prevent damage to the screw and driver.

CROWBAR—for pulling pallets apart and other pieces of joined wood that need to come apart, a crowbar or pry bar is used as a lever either to force apart two objects or to remove nails.

PINCERS—used in many situations where a mechanical advantage is required to pinch, cut, or pull an object.

COMBINATION PLIERS—the primary purpose of pliers is usually to provide a tight grip, or grip things it would be difficult

to hold with your fingers, allowing you to bend, twist, pull, or otherwise manipulate a material. I mainly use combination (linesman) pliers, an all-round tool good for almost any job around the house.

CHISEL—looks a bit like a thick flat-head screwdriver. Combined with a hammer, use it to make recesses in wood (see the Play Tent project on page 72). I also use it to take pieces of wood apart.

ABOVE Nail gun.
BELOW LEFT Hammers.
BELOW MIDDLE Flat-head and cross-head screwdrivers.
BELOW RIGHT Crowbar, pincers, and pliers.

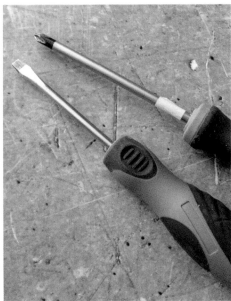

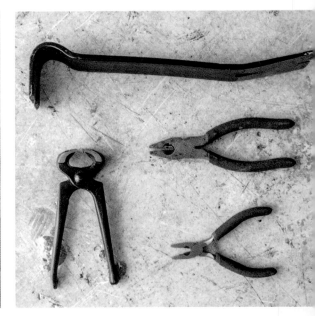

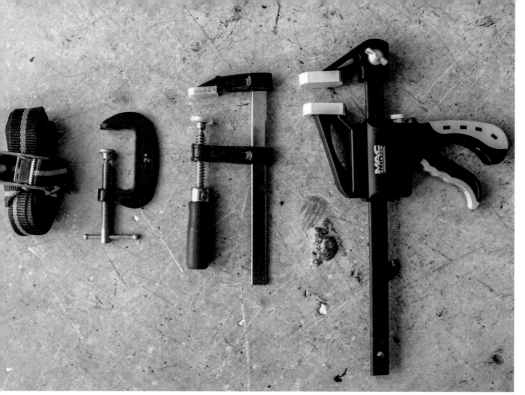

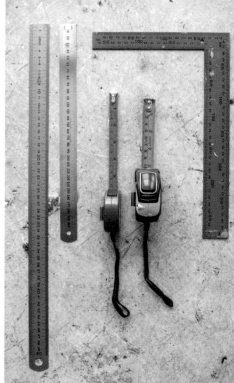

CLAMPS—make cutting wood safer and more accurate by clamping it in place when you cut it. Also use clamps to keep joints together when waiting for glue to dry. There are several different kinds.

C-clamps (sometimes also called G-clamps) are light-duty clamps sufficient for most jobs around the house. The top of the "C" usually has a small flat edge. At the bottom is a threaded hole through which a large threaded screw can be turned to tighten the wood in place. You can buy these clamps in many sizes—my most used ones are 2 inches (50mm) and 4¾ inches (120mm).

F-clamps have a wider opening capacity than a C-clamp, plus a fixed jaw and a large screw on the lower bar that allows for the clamp to be tightened. When using a soft wood, put an extra plank in between the clamp to prevent the screw jaw from marking the wood. I mainly use an 8¼-inch (21-cm) clamp.

Belt clamps are for clamping large or oddly shaped pieces. The flexible nylon strap secures your wood and the ratcheting mechanism in the clasp makes it easy to tighten and release the clamp.

One-handed bar clamps are tightened and released with just one hand, making them very popular with any DIY-er. They typically have one sliding jaw and one fixed jaw. Simply squeeze the handle to tighten in place. The jaws are big and flat, minimizing the chances of marking the wood. Sizes available range from 6 inches (15cm) upward—I mainly use my 12-inch (30-cm) and 20-inch (50-cm) ones.

ABOVE LEFT Belt clamp, C-clamp, F-clamp, and one-handed bar clamp.
ABOVE RIGHT My rulers—metal, retractable, and a corner square.

WORK BENCH—when using (power) tools, it is very important that you have a flat and stable surface to work on. I love using my Workmate as it's foldable, adjustable, and of a good height, so time spent constructing projects doesn't become back-breaking work. The tabletop consists of two sturdy wooden jaws, one of which is fixed and the other able to be moved in and out so it can be used as a bench vice to hold wood and other items while working on them. Also see my Work Bench project on page 34.

VICE—I like to use a vice when working on a small piece of wood that I can't hold in my hands to sand or drill. Also great for holding pieces that need painting.

MEASURING RULE—an absolutely essential piece of kit. I like to use a long retractable rule plus a solid metal ruler.

CORNER SQUARE, CARPENTER'S SQUARE, AND TRI-SQUARE—L-shaped metal pieces that help ensure a corner is straight and at a 90-degree angle. Ideal for adding legs to tables and hanging shelves on a wall. Hold one side against the edge of the material so the blade is positioned at a 90-degree angle compared to the edge, line the other piece of wood (like the table leg) up to the other side, and screw in place.

HARDWARE

SCREWS—the most common connectors, providing a strong wood-to-wood connection. I have used wood screws throughout this book as they have a sharp point which easily drives through wood. Keep a selection of different lengths in your tool box.

NAILS—these provide a quick connection but are not as strong as screws. I like using nails when I want the nail head to show. Finishing nails have such a small head that you will hardly notice them in your build. If using a nail gun, you use collated framing nails—strips of nails held together by paper or plastic.

NUTS AND BOLTS—used together, with the bolt running all the way through the wood and secured on the other end with a nut or cap.

BRACKETS—metal braces with pre-drilled holes that will instantly increase the strength of your structure. Also great for adding legs to a piece without the need to screw through the main surface.

HINGES—used for the Fold-down Window Table project on page 22, allowing the tabletop to fold flat against the wall.

BOTTOM LEFT Various sizes of screws, nails, nuts, and bolts.

BOTTOM MIDDLE Corner brackets are useful to have in your tool kit to strengthen your builds.

BOTTOM RIGHT Selection of hinges.

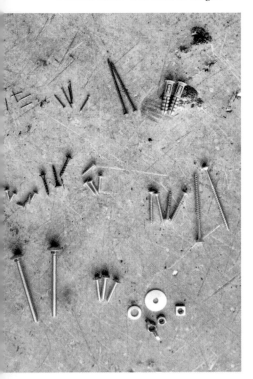

BASIC TECHNIQUES

MEASURING

Adopt the old saying "measure twice and cut once" as your mantra. Make sure to have the correct measurements before setting the saw into your wood. I use a combination of a metal ruler and a retractable one. Mark where you need to cut your wood with a pencil as the mark is easily removed if you make a mistake (you'll see me marking with a pen in some of the step-by-step photos but that is only because pencil marks don't always show up in photos).

CUTTING

Using a handsaw—using a pencil, mark where your cut needs to be and place your saw blade just on the outside of that line (you lose a very tiny amount of wood to sawdust and you don't want your wood to end up a little short). I don't like to have my hands anywhere near a sharp blade, so I start off making very small saw movements until I have a notch the saw blade fits into neatly. You can then start making bigger strokes, keeping your saw at a 45-degree angle. Don't press on the saw—let the blade do the work.

Using a jigsaw—make sure to have a stable work surface (such as a work bench, table, or a Workmate) and always have the wood clamped in place so it will not move during sawing. Remember that the wood you want to cut has to overhang the edge of your work surface. Fit the saw with the correct blade for the material you want to cut. Press the saw down on the wood, start the motor, and guide the blade just on the outside edge of your marked line (remembering you lose a tiny amount of wood to sawdust—see above). Move the saw forward at a pace that allows the blade to cut the wood without deflecting; don't try to push the jigsaw forward. Switch off the saw before moving it away from the wood.

Using a circular saw—as with the jigsaw, make sure to have a stable work surface and remember that the wood to be cut must overhang the work surface. Set the blade to the correct depth of the wood you want to cut, line the saw up with the outside edge of your cutline (remembering you lose a tiny amount of wood to sawdust—see above). Look at the front of the saw at the guide notch and keep the notch lined up with the pencil line for a straight cut. Switch on the motor and start cutting, making sure to keep the base of the saw flat on the wood. Push the saw into the wood with enough force to move it forward, but not so hard that the motor speed seems to decrease. When your cut has been made, switch off the motor and wait for the blade to stop spinning before moving your saw away from the wood.

Using an electric miter saw—make sure your saw is sitting on a stable work surface. Set your saw to the correct angle you want to cut the wood at. Put your wood on the cutting surface, pushing it against the backrest of the saw's bench. When the cutline is in the correct place, clamp your wood tightly in position either with the saw's clamp or a separate one. Longer pieces of wood can be held in place with the hand that is not

SAW SAFETY

THESE RULES ALSO APPLY WHEN USING OTHER POWER TOOLS.

• ALWAYS UNPLUG THE SAW BEFORE CHANGING THE BLADE.

• ALWAYS PUSH UP LOOSE-FITTING SLEEVES, TIE LONG HAIR UP, AND DON'T WEAR LONG NECKLACES OR SCARVES, OR ANYTHING WHICH COULD BECOME CAUGHT UP IN THE TOOL.

• WEAR SAFETY GLASSES TO PROTECT YOUR EYES FROM SAWDUST AND SPLINTERS, A DUST MASK, AND EAR PROTECTORS TO PRESERVE YOUR HEARING.

• LET THE BLADE COME TO A COMPLETE STOP AT THE END OF A CUT BEFORE LIFTING THE SAW.

• NEVER REACH UNDER THE SAW WHEN THE BLADE IS ROTATING, EVEN IF IT HAS A GUARD.

• ALWAYS CLAMP YOUR WOOD IN PLACE SO THAT IT DOESN'T MOVE WHILE CUTTING.

• ALWAYS FOLLOW THE MANUFACTURER'S INSTRUCTIONS AND SAFETY GUIDELINES.

• YOU MIGHT WANT TO PRACTICE USING A POWER TOOL ON A SPARE OFFCUT OF WOOD FIRST.

LEFT Sanding with a palm sander.
BELOW LEFT Pilot holes and pre-drilling.
BELOW RIGHT Countersinking.

Electric palm sander—attach the correct grid of paper to the underside of your sander, making sure the holes match up. Press the sander down on your wood, switch it on, and move the sander back and forth across the grain of the wood. Don't apply too much pressure—let the pad do the work.

DRILLING PILOT HOLES AND PRE-DRILLING

Pilot holes—you drill small pilot holes using a small drill bit to prevent the wood from splitting. Pilot holes make it easier for a bigger drill bit to go through the wood or to make it easier to hammer a nail in place. I drill very small holes around the edge of the wood where the nails need to go, so I have to use less force when hammering the nails in place. Make sure to do this with a very thin drill bit smaller then the nail. If you need to drill a big hole, first drill a pilot hole using a small drill bit and then change up to a bigger sized drill bit.

Pilot holes for screws or pre-drilling—pre-drill a small hole to help when screwing in screws and to prevent the wood from splitting. The correct pre-drilled size is slightly smaller than your screw size (there are handy size charts available online).

Countersinking—when you countersink, you make the first bit of a pre-drilled hole bigger so when the screw is in the wood, the screw head will sit flush or below the surface of the wood. You can then fill the hole with filler, making the screw invisible. I like to use a special drill piece for this, but you could just use a drill bit with a bigger circumference.

GLUING

I use a lot of wood glue in this book. Whenever you join two pieces of wood together and you want the bond to be strong and lasting, add a bit of wood glue. Apply evenly over the surface and let set for the specified time on your bottle of glue. Most are hard within 24 hours and clamp-dry (i.e. when you can take the clamps off) in half an hour. My favorite glue used in this book is Gorilla wood glue.

USING CLAMPS

Clamps are used when you want to hold two pieces together, perhaps if you have glued wood together and are waiting for the glue to set, or to hold a piece of wood in place when cutting. Twist or push the clamps as tightly around the wood as possible.

operating the saw—but always keep your hand far away from the blade! To start a cut, squeeze the trigger and wait for the saw to reach maximum rotation. Then slowly lower the saw into the wood. Never force the saw through the wood. Let the saw cut and then guide it downward. Once you have completed the cut, bring the saw back up and out of the wood, then release the trigger and put the saw back in its original position.

SANDING

Sandpaper—rub this over cut edges to get rid of any splinters, over the surface of wood to remove varnish or a thin coat of paint, to prep the wood before painting, and to make the surface super-smooth to the touch.

USING WOOD FILLER

Fills the screw holes you created with countersinking and any cracks in the joints or wood that aren't supposed to be there. Use a putty knife to push the filler in place, let set, then smooth over with sandpaper once dry. You can buy white filler and ones that are colored to match the wood you are using.

OILING

Oil is one of the most popular ways to finish wood, as it will protect it and enhance its natural beauty. You use an oil on wood to seal the surface and make it less absorbent, so that it can be used for food and washed afterward (when oiling wood that will come in contact with food, always use a food-grade oil, i.e. a non-toxic oil that is food-safe, like mineral oil or tung oil). The oil will penetrate into the surface of the wood, unlike a varnish that will sit on top. Always follow the instructions on the bottle. Oils are very easy to apply—just use a lint-free cloth, let the oil dry, and apply a second coat if needed.

PAINTING

Give your project a whole new look with a lick of paint. I like to use furniture paints for a splash of color or chalk paint for a matt feel. Make sure the surface is clean and dust-free, stir your paint with a stirring stick, then apply your first coat and let dry. Apply a second coat if needed. In this book I only used water-based paints as they are a lot easier to use and dry quickly. Oil-based paints, like gloss paint, are more durable but take a long time to dry; they also require white spirit to clean the brush.

To make paint last on outdoor pieces, coat the painted wood with an outdoor varnish to make it water- and weatherproof. You can buy varnish in a matt, satin (soft sheen), or silk (high sheen) finish.

DRILLING HOLES IN A WALL

You might be able to hang your wall build directly from the studwork using wood screws, but if you have a solid wall made from brick, you will have to drill a hole with a masonry drill bit first. Always check there are no hidden wires or pipes in your wall first before you make the cut. You can do this using a special wall detector tool. Using a masonry drill bit the same width as your wall plug, drill your hole deep enough to accommodate the plug (I like to mark the drill bit with a bit of masking tape to the right depth). Push your wall plug or rawl plug in the hole (it might need a bit of help from a hammer), and screw your screw in place.

FOLLOWING THE PROJECT INSTRUCTIONS

All measurements given in the projects are for guidance, as you will probably have to adjust them to suit the pallet wood you are working with. Use my instructions as a "recipe," adjusting it to suit your ingredients, and feel free to deviate. You can also use my builds as inspiration and build something that fits in your home perfectly. Finally, only use one set of measurements (I have provided both Imperial and metric) as they are not interchangeable.

No two pallets are the same, so all the measurements given in the projects are for the wood I used—you need to adapt them for your build to suit the wood you have. In most projects I talk about the width of your wood to make the instructions a bit easier. When selecting planks for your build, it's easiest if all your planks are of the same width. Pallet planks are normally between 2¾ and 3¼ inches (7 and 8cm) wide. The thickness might vary too. Pallet wood is almost never straight, so discard any very warped planks or use these for small projects. If you are a fan of neat, straight lines in your builds, pallet wood might not be the material for you! When you build with pallet wood, all your builds will have a slightly rustic look.

CHAPTER 1

PALLET FURNITURE

FOLD-DOWN WINDOW TABLE

The perfect spot for a cup of coffee with a friend! Build this table under a window and you can use it as your own little barista station—just keep passing those coffees through the open window! When the table isn't in use, take the legs away and fold the table flat against the wall. My table was made to fit my window's size, but you can adjust the size to suit your chosen window.

YOU WILL NEED:

Pallet wood planks—
I used 10

Measuring rule

Saw

Palm sander

Drill driver with wood drill bit and countersink bit

Wood screws

Wood glue

Nail gun or hammer and nails

2 butt hinges, 4 inches (100mm) in length

1 For the tabletop, select seven planks that look good together and cut them to the same length—mine are 42 inches (107cm) long to fit below my window frame. Sand the planks smooth. Place five of these planks good side down and butted up next to each other, then measure how deep your tabletop is, from front to back (set aside the two remaining prepared planks, for use in step 3). From the unused pallet planks, cut three planks to this measurement minus 2 inches (5cm). For me, this is 15 - 2 = 13 inches (38 - 5 = 33cm)—these are the support planks which go below the tabletop.

2 Screw the three support planks to the reverse side of the tabletop, placing them equidistantly from the edges with one in the center and the other two 2 inches (15cm) in from the outer edges. Turn the tabletop right side up and give it a final blast with the sander.

3 The two remaining planks prepared in step 1 make the back piece which attaches the table to the wall. In one of the planks drill four equidistant ¼-inch (4-mm) holes to hang the plank from the wall, countersinking the holes so the screws will disappear.

4 Place the remaining prepared plank on top of the one with the holes to form an L-shape. Make sure the countersunk holes face forward (you will screw through these to attach the table to the wall later). Glue and then nail the pieces together.

5 To make the notches which hold the legs in place, from a scrap of pallet wood cut four pieces, each ¾ inch (2cm) long.

6 Glue and screw two pieces to the underside of the second plank from the front of the tabletop. Allow enough space between them to slot in a leg formed from another pallet plank. These pieces are narrow so pre-drill the holes before you screw.

7 To make the legs, cut two planks to the height of your window minus the thickness of your tabletop. For me, this is 35 - ¾ = 34¼ inches (89 - 2 = 87cm). Sand the planks.

8 Take the L-shaped piece you made in step 4 and attach the two hinges to the plank without the countersunk holes. Position the hinges 1¼ inches (3cm) in from the ends, lining the hinge up with the edge of the wood.

9 Line the tabletop up with the L-shaped back piece and screw the other side of the hinge to the underside of the table top.

10 Using the countersunk holes, screw the back piece into your wall, so the tabletop folds down flat against the wall. To use, lift the tabletop up and slot the legs into place.

GARDEN CHAIR

This chair looks very impressive in your garden, but all you need for it is some plywood, pallet wood planks, and a few tools. Your friends will be so impressed when you say you made it yourself! The dimensions given are for a chair for a small garden, but add 4 or 8 inches (10 or 20cm) to every measurement to create a medium or large chair. Now all I need is a pretty deck, a drink, and a nice view, and you won't see me for the rest of the weekend!

YOU WILL NEED:

Outdoor plywood, 71 x 24-inch (180 x 60-cm) sheet, ¾ inch (18mm) thick

Pallet wood planks— I used 12

Pencil

Measuring rule

Jigsaw

Palm sander

Saw

Drill driver with ¼-inch (4-mm) wood drill bit and countersink bit

1½-inch (40-mm) wood screws

Spirit level

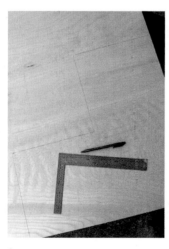

1 To make the side piece, on your plywood draw an L-shape to the following dimensions: back is 27½ inches (70cm) high, front is 12 inches (30cm) high, and 24 inches (60cm) wide at the base. The top is 12 inches (30cm) wide and the seat back is 12 inches (30cm) long.

2 Soften the top and bottom corners at the front of the chair. I drew with a Sharpie so it shows up better in the photo but you should use a pencil so you can rub it out and adjust the lines as necessary.

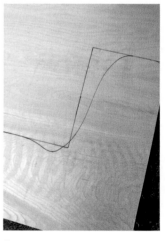

3 Now shape the backrest by giving it a nice curve at the top and draw a little dip in the seat.

4 Cut out your shape with a jigsaw, then sand the cut edges smooth. You now have one side of the chair.

5 Use this cut-out piece as a template—place it on the remaining piece of the plywood sheet and trace around it, then cut it out and sand the edges.

6 To make the slats, cut your pallet wood planks into lengths of 18 inches (45cm). Cut these planks in half widthwise. Sand the cut edges. My chair used 51 slats, but the total number of slats depends on how closely you fit them. Drill a ¼-inch (4-mm) hole at each end of each slat, ½ inch (1cm) in from the edge and in the center.

7 Screw the slats to both plywood sides with the wood screws, leaving small, equidistant gaps between the slats. It's important to make sure the slats are horizontal, so use a spirit level to check the first few are correct.

8 Keep going until the entire chair is covered with slats, including the base.

9 Sand the chair smooth using a fine-grid sandpaper.

MOSAIC INLAY TABLE

Turn a pallet into a table with the simple addition of four table legs. The ones I used are from Ikea and you just screw them in under the pallet, so you can make a table in just a few minutes! The one drawback was the gaps between the slats—I would find it very annoying to have to take care where I place my glass so I closed them up with a fun mosaic inlay. This adds a great color detail to a plain table and makes the pallet even more functional.

YOU WILL NEED:

Half a pallet (you can cut a full-sized one in half)

Plywood

Saw

Palm sander or sandpaper

Paint and paintbrush

Measuring rule

Drill driver with wood drill bit

Screws

4 table legs—I used Hilver from Ikea

Tiles—I used around 10 tiles from Topps Tiles

Hammer

Safety goggles and gloves

Old towel

Tile adhesive

Tile grout and spatula

Sponge or cloth

1 Sand your half pallet as smooth as you can. I then added a spalsh of water to my Annie Sloan Chalk Paint® in Pure to give the pallet a white wash. It's nice to still see the wood grain, but you can use gloss paint if you want a more modern look.

2 Measure the inside dimensions of the underside of the pallet on each side of the central strut and cut two pieces of plywood to size. Screw in place to close the tabletop.

3 Screw the table legs to the base. You have a nice table now and this could be a quick build, but I prefer having the gaps between the slats built up to the same level so that plates and glasses don't topple over.

4 To make the mosaic inlay, smash up some tiles with a hammer. Make sure to wear safety goggles and gloves, and wrap an old towel around the tiles before hitting them with the hammer, to stop sharp shards flying everywhere.

5 Use the tile adhesive to stick the tile pieces to the plywood between the pallet slats, making sure the tiles are at the same level as the pallet wood surface. If the gaps are too deep and you would have to use too much adhesive to reach the pallet level, fill the gaps with some wood offcuts and fix the tiles on top. Let dry overnight or until the adhesive is completely dry.

6 Apply grout between the tile pieces—I pressed mine in place with a flexible spatula. Scrape any excess grout off the wood.

7 Let the grout dry for 15 minutes (or follow the manufacturer's instructions), then clean any smears of grout off the tiles and wood for a nice clean finish.

DECK CHAIR

After building all the projects in this book, what better way to relax by the pool or in the garden than in your hand-built deck chair? The wheels under the frame make this chair very easy to move around the terrace, so you can chase the sun or shade.

YOU WILL NEED:

Outdoor treated wood, 1¾ x 1¾ inches (4.5 x 4.5cm), for the legs, painted white

Outdoor treated wood, 1¾ x ¾ inches (4.5 x 2cm), for the back supports, painted white

Pallet wood planks

Measuring rule

Saw

Miter saw or handsaw with miter box

Palm sander or sandpaper

Drill driver with wood drill bit

Wood glue

Four 2½-inch (65-mm) wood screws

Twenty 1¼-inch (30-mm) wood screws

Eight ¾-inch (20-mm) wood screws

Two ³⁄₈-inch (8-mm) bolts with washers and wing nuts

2 caster wheels, no bigger than 1¾ x 1¾ inches (4.5 x 4.5cm)

White paint and paintbrush

1 For the short front legs, cut the 1¾ x 1¾-inch (4.5 x 4.5-cm) wood 6¼ inches (16cm) long with one end cut at a 20-degree angle. For the longer back legs, cut two more pieces 35½ inches (90cm) long with straight ends.

2 To attach the short front legs to the longer back legs, pre-drill two holes through the back legs ½ and 1¼ inches (1 and 3cm) from one edge (think of how two dots look on a dice—that's the position of these holes). Glue and screw the angled ends of the front legs under the frame, making sure that the angled ends of the front legs slope down and inward. Use 2½-inch (65-mm) screws.

3 For the seat, cut six pallet wood planks 20 inches (50cm) long and sand smooth. Glue and screw five of these planks to the legs, with the front plank overhanging the front legs a little. Use the 1¼-inch (30-mm) wood screws and pre-drill the holes to prevent the pallet wood splitting. (Reserve the sixth plank to use in step 8.)

4 To make the back support, from the 1¾ x ¾-inch (4.5 x 2-cm) wood cut two pieces 20 inches (50cm) long. In each piece, drill a ³/₈-inch (8-mm) hole ¾ inch (2cm) from one end, pre-drilling a smaller hole first to prevent the wood splitting.

5 Drill a hole of the same size in the long legs, ¾ inch (2cm) away from the last seat plank.

6 Line the back supports up with the chair and push a bolt through the holes. On the inside of the chair put a washer and wing nut around the bolt and twist tight.

7 For the chair back, cut four pallet wood planks 16½ inches (41.5cm) long and sand smooth. Glue and screw to the backrest. Use the 1¼-inch (30-mm) wood screws and pre-drill the holes to prevent the wood splitting.

8 Set the backrest at a comfortable angle (loosen the bolt, adjust the angle, and then re-tighten the nut). Glue and screw the reserved seat plank behind the back supports (this keeps the back in place).

9 Screw the wheels to the front legs of the chair, using the ¾-inch (20-mm) screws. Touch up the cut edges of the chair frame with a dab of white paint.

WORK BENCH

Perfect for your shed, workshop, or summerhouse, this work bench is made from old scaffolding boards, meaning it is very sturdy and hardwearing. I use the bench for all my planting and DIYing, and the shelf at the bottom is handy for storage. If you wish, make the top and the shelf from pallet wood and use as a display table. As I'm tall, I made my bench 39 inches (100cm) high, but you can make the legs shorter for a bench with a more average height of 35½ inches (90cm). If you prefer sitting while you work, make the bench 29½ inches (75cm) high.

YOU WILL NEED:

2 fence posts, 3 x 3 inches (7.5 x 7.5cm) and 78 inches (200cm) long

4 pieces of 1½ x ¾-inch (4 x 2-cm) white wood, each 94 inches (240cm) long

2 scaffolding boards, 8¾ inches (22cm) wide and 1³⁄₈ inches (3.5cm) thick, 117 inches (300cm) long

Measuring rule

Saw

Palm sander

Drill driver with wood drill bit and countersink bit

2½-inch (65-mm) and 1½-inch (40-mm) wood screws

4 corner brackets

Hammer and chisel

Jigsaw

1 To make the bench legs, cut each fence post in half, to make four lengths of 39 inches (100cm), then sand all rough edges. Cut the white wood as follows, then sand all rough edges:

- Four 51-inch (130-cm) lengths
- Two 16-inch (40-cm) lengths
- Two 14-inch (36-cm) lengths
- Four 6½-inch (17-cm) lengths

2 Screw two of the long pieces of white wood to the top of the fence posts using the larger wood screws and placing the white wood so it will be on the outer edges of the fence posts. Screw the 16-inch (40-cm) short sides to the outer edges of the top of the fence posts, completing the frame for the bench top.

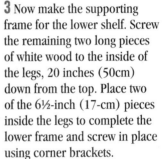

3 Now make the supporting frame for the lower shelf. Screw the remaining two long pieces of white wood to the inside of the legs, 20 inches (50cm) down from the top. Place two of the 6½-inch (17-cm) pieces inside the legs to complete the lower frame and screw in place using corner brackets.

4 In both the upper and lower frames, drill pilot holes 16 and 36 inches (40 and 90cm) from one end and countersink. Screw the 14-inch (36-cm) batons in between the top frame and the remaining 6½-inch (17-cm) pieces in between the lower frame, using the smaller wood screws.

5 Cut the scaffolding boards to two lengths of 67 inches (170cm) for the top and two lengths of 51 inches (130cm) for the lower shelf, then sand the cut ends. Cut one of the 51-inch (130-cm) pieces to 5½ inches (14cm) wide. On the 51-inch (130-cm) pieces use a hammer and chisel to remove the metal band from the ends of the planks. (If you wish, the shelf could be made from pallet wood.)

6 On the planks for the lower shelf, you will need to fit the wood around the legs by cutting a 3-inch (7.5-cm) notch from the outer corners of the 51-inch (130-cm) pieces. Mark where you need to cut, then use a jigsaw to remove the square. Sand the cut edges.

7 Push the shelving planks in place. You may need to use the hammer to force them in if the fit is tight—never hit the wood itself, but use a scrap piece to protect the shelf from hammer marks.

8 Drill pilot holes, countersink, and screw the shelving planks to the frame using the larger wood screws.

9 Place the 67-inch (170-cm) boards on the top frame, making sure to have an equal overhang on each side. I made the back flush with the frame, with an overhang only at the front of the bench. Drill pilot holes, countersink, and screw the wood to the frame using the larger wood screws. Use a palm sander to sand the work surface smooth.

Work Bench

COLOR POP BENCH

If you have a few spare planks of pallet wood, this bench is a brilliantly simple project and will make a lovely addition to your garden. The bright yellow side provides a great color pop on a cloudy day.

YOU WILL NEED:

Pallet wood planks of the same width—I used 9

Outdoor treated wood, 1¾ x ¾ inch (45 x18mm)

Measuring rule

Saw

Palm sander

Wood glue

Nail gun or hammer and nails

Clamps

Drill driver with ⅜-inch (8-mm) wood drill bit

Six 2¼-inch (60-mm) deck screws

Paint and paintbrush

Matt outdoor varnish

Ten ¾-inch (20-mm) wood screws

Three ⅜-inch (8-mm) bolts with washers and nuts

1 To make the seat, cut six pallet planks to the same length— mine are 40½ inches (103cm) as that was the length of my shortest plank. Sand them smooth. Glue and then nail two planks together to make a thicker, stronger plank, so you end up with three planks, each of double thickness.

2 Line up your three planks, wrong sides facing up. Apply wood glue to the long edges of the middle plank and clamp the three planks together. Measure the total width of the planks— for me, this is 9¼ inches (23.5cm)—and cut two pieces of pallet wood to this length. Glue and screw these 4 inches (10cm) in from the ends.

3 To make the wooden end of the bench, cut six pieces of pallet wood, each 16 inches (40cm) long. Glue and nail these to form three planks of double thickness, as in step 1. Then measure a single piece of wood to the same width and attach it 4 inches (10cm) from one end, as in step 2.

4 On one end of the bench seat, pre-drill six holes ½ inch (1cm) in from the edge.

5 Glue and screw the side piece to the seat, using 2¼-inch (60-mm) deck screws. Make sure that the horizontal piece spanning the planks is on the inside of the bench and farthest from the seat.

6 Now make the frame for the other end of the bench, using the outdoor treated wood. For the two horizontal pieces, measure the width of the bench plus twice the thickness of the outdoor wood—for me, this is 9¼ + ¾ + ¾ = 10¾ inches (23.5cm + 18mm + 18mm = 27.1cm). For the two uprights, measure the wood end of your bench, add the thickness of the seat, then deduct the thickness of the outdoor wood—for me, this is 16 + 1½ - ¾ = 16¾ inches (40cm + 3.8cm − 18mm = 42cm).

7 Paint your frame pieces— I used Annie Sloan Chalk Paint® in English Yellow, followed by a coat of matt outdoor varnish.

8 Pre-drill holes in the shorter, horizontal pieces, in the middle of the ends and ½ inch (1cm) in from the edge. Glue and then screw the frame together with the ¾-inch (20-mm) wood screws.

9 Measure and then drill three ³/₈-inch (8-mm) holes evenly spread across the top of the frame.

10 Clamp the frame in place around the bench, 3 inches (7.5cm) in from the end, and drill through the pre-drilled holes into the seat of the bench.

11 Attach the frame to the bench with the bolts, securing them in place with a washer and nut on the underside of the bench seat. Paint the outer screw heads with a dab of yellow paint to hide them.

OUTDOOR SOFA

I like to spend a lot of time outdoors and this bench on my decking is the perfect spot for relaxing, for a quick break with a cup of coffee and a magazine, or a long, lazy lunch with a group of friends. As you can see overleaf, my little dog Kermit is a big fan of the sofa too, and he loves to sunbathe in his favorite corner. This sofa is made from two separate benches pushed together to create an L-shape—this makes it easier to build and a lot easier to move.

THE SOFA IS BUILT FROM DECKING BOARDS WHICH WERE LEFT OVER AFTER BUILDING MY TERRACE, BUT YOU COULD EASILY USE PALLET WOOD AS LONG AS IT IS SANDED SMOOTH. YOU WILL NEED TO USE TWO PIECES OF PALLET WOOD ALONG THE TOP (RATHER THAN ONE LONG PIECE OF WOOD) WITH THE ENDS MEETING ON THE MIDDLE FRAME SO YOU CAN SECURE IT IN PLACE THERE. THIS IS A VERY SIMPLE DESIGN AND YOU WILL HAVE IT COMPLETED IN A COUPLE OF HOURS.

MAKE THE BENCH AS LONG AS YOU WANT TO FIT YOUR GARDEN OR DECKING. THE BIG BENCH HERE IS 86½ INCHES (220CM) LONG AND THE LITTLE ONE IS 39 INCHES (100CM). I MADE MY BENCH FOUR PLANK WIDTHS HIGH—IT SAVES YOU A LOT OF SAWING IF YOU GO WITH THE EXISTING WIDTH OF YOUR PLANKS.

YOU WILL NEED:

Outdoor timber for the frame, 2 x 2 inches (5 x 5cm) and long enough for the number of frames you need to construct

Decking boards, 4¾ x ¾ inches (12 x 2cm) and at least 86½ inches (220cm) long

Measuring rule

Saw

Drill driver with wood drill bit

¾-inch (40-mm) wood screws

Palm sander or sandpaper

1 Build the frames. You need one frame at each end and one every 31 inches (80cm) along the length of the bench. My big bench has four frames and my little bench just two. For each frame, cut two pieces of wood 19 inches (48cm) long (or the combined height of your planks) and two pieces of wood 19 inches (48cm) minus twice the thickness of the wood—in my case, the wood is 2 inches (5cm) thick, so this was 19 - 2 - 2 = 15 inches (48 - 5 - 5 = 38cm).

2 Screw together to create square frames, pre-drilling the screw holes first to make it easier for you and to prevent the wood splitting.

3 Saw the decking boards to the length of your benches and attach to the two frames, pre-drilling the holes and screwing in place with wood screws. Make sure to have an overhang the thickness of the wood at each end. If your bench requires more than one support frame, screw these in place too.

4 Cut the side pieces to the right length and screw to the sides of the frame. On my little bench I only closed off one side as the other side will be pushed against the big bench and won't be seen. Sand any rough edges.

5 Turn the bench onto its back, so the front is facing upward. Cut the remaining boards to the correct length and screw in place to complete the front of the bench.

AS MY BENCH IS PLACED AGAINST A WALL I DIDN'T NEED TO COVER THE BACK OF THE FRAME. IF YOUR BENCH IS FREESTANDING, REPEAT STEP 3 FOR THE BACK, TOO.

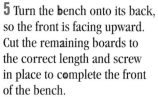

COLORFUL FOOTSTOOL

I love looking for old weathered wood, especially painted pieces which have a great patina that has built up over the years, but did you know you can successfully fake that look? I painted the planks of this stool before building it and sanded off most of the paint to create instant patina! The size of this stool makes it super-handy to have around the garden, perfect to perch on, to rest your feet, to have as a child's seat, or to use as a side table.

YOU WILL NEED:

Sanded pallet wood planks—I used 6

Scrap pieces of ¾ x 1½-inch (2 x 4-cm) white wood, total length of 24 inches (60cm)

Paint and paintbrush or cloth

Piece of cardboard

Measuring rule

Pencil

Scissors

Saw

Palm sander or sandpaper

Drill driver with wood drill bit

Wood glue

Wood screws

Nail gun or hammer and nails

Matt outdoor varnish (optional)

1 Roughly paint your pallet wood planks—I used Annie Sloan Chalk Paint® in Provence, Emile, Henrietta, and Giverny. I used a cloth to rub the paint on, but you could use a paintbrush. I deliberately applied the paint roughly and left a few bare spots—you don't want the finish to be too neat.

2 Make a template for the stool legs from a piece of cardboard. Draw a rectangle measuring 10 x 3¼ inches (25 x 8cm). Make a mark in the center of the bottom short side and another mark 3¼ inches (8cm) down from the top in the right corner. Draw an angled line to connect the two marks and cut out your template.

3 Trace the template onto your painted wood, four times with the tapered corner facing to the right and four times facing to the left.

4 Cut out the eight legs and sand the cut sides smooth.

5 From the offcuts of the painted pallet planks, cut four pieces measuring 3½ inches (9cm) in length. These are the pieces that will sit between the tops of the legs. Line up two legs and a middle piece and check the overall width—for me, this is 9 inches (23cm).

6 From the white wood, cut the inner frame—cut two pieces that match the width of the two legs and middle piece measured in step 5, i.e. 9 inches (23cm). Also cut two pieces that are the width minus the frame thickness and minus twice the thickness of the wood—for me, this is 9 - ¾ - 2¼ = 6 inches (23 - 2 - 6 = 15cm). Pre-drill a screw hole in the middle of the longer pieces, ½ inch (1cm) from the side.

7 Glue and then screw the square frame together.

8 Glue and nail the legs and middle pieces to the outside of the frame. Make sure that the angled sides of the legs face in.

9 From the remaining painted planks, cut four planks, each measuring 10¼ inches (26cm). Glue and nail these to the top of the stool. My measurements allowed for a ¾-inch (2-cm) overhang on all four sides, but you can make this more or less depending on the width of your planks.

10 Apply dabs of paint to the cut sides of the legs and let dry, then use a palm sander to distress the paint more if needed. Add a coat of matt outdoor varnish if you plan to keep the stool outside all year round.

CHEVRON TABLE

A perfect spot to do your work outside, this pallet wood writing desk isn't just for your summer house, terrace, or shed—it is good enough to make it into your home! The tabletop looks complicated, but if you have a miter saw it is so easy to build. The mint-green hairpin legs give a nice color pop to the build.

YOU WILL NEED:

Outdoor plywood, 35½ x 20 inches (90 x 50cm), ¾ inch (19mm) thick

Pallet wood planks, sanded smooth

Measuring rule

Pencil

Miter saw or handsaw with miter box

Saw

Wood glue

Nail gun or hammer and nails

Palm sander

Four hairpin legs—mine are from The Hairpin Leg Company

Drill driver

1-inch (25-mm) wood screws

Wood oil and lint-free cloth

IF YOU DON'T HAVE A MITER SAW, USE A PENCIL TO TRACE THE WOOD WHERE YOU NEED TO CUT AND USE A HANDSAW TO TRIM TO SIZE.

1 On your piece of plywood draw a line down the center, dividing it into two halves, each 10 inches (25cm) wide.

2 Using a miter saw or miter box, cut two right-angled triangles from pallet wood. The long sides are 6 inches (15cm), with both ends cut at a 45-degree angle but facing opposite ways. Place the triangles on the plywood, lining them up with the line drawn down the middle.

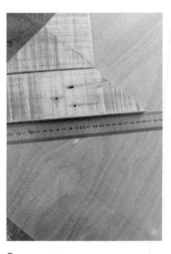

3 Measure how long your next piece needs to be. I like using a scrap piece of wood for this (with the end cut on a 45-degree angle) as it does not matter if it doesn't reach the table edge—butt the scrap wood next to the first triangle and measure the length of the far side from the central line to the edge of the table. Cut this from a plank of pallet wood.

4 If you don't have a miter saw, place a piece of wood with a 45-degree cut end on the straight line and mark where you need to cut it to line up with the edge of the table.

5 Keep going until you have several pallet wood pieces cut. The first three pieces, or until you have cleared the corner, will be trapeziums (angles going opposite ways). When you have cleared the corner, the pieces have corners going in the same direction, so you can use a piece as a template to cut enough wood to cover the table.

6 Lift a triangle of wood carefully off the table. Apply wood glue to the underside and place it back in position on the plywood. Repeat with the other triangle and then with the next pieces of wood. It is important to butt them up closely so that the edges all line up. After gluing, nail the wood to the plywood base using a nail gun or hammer and nails.

7 Keep going with cutting, gluing, and nailing until the whole tabletop is covered. When you reach the other end of the table, mark where you have to cut the overhang (as in step 4).

8 The last pieces will be triangles, filling in the outer corners of the table (you may have to trim a little off the right angle to make them fit). Glue and nail in place.

9 Cut four pallet planks to make the trim around the sides. You need two planks the length of the table and two planks the width of the table plus twice the thickness of the wood. Glue and nail the trim in place, lining up one edge with the tabletop and letting the lower edge hang below the tabletop.

10 Sand the tabletop and the edging trim, making sure you get a really smooth and even surface.

11 Attach the four table legs to the underside of the table with the screws.

12 To bring out the wood grain and really show off the difference in the pallet wood planks, use a wood oil on the planks. I used a teak oil, rubbed on with a lint-free cloth.

PALLET SOFAS

It doesn't take much to turn a pallet into a great sofa base. If you really want to rough it, you don't have to do anything more than throw some pillows on top! However, I upscaled my pallets by adding little legs and painting them a deep inky blue. This project is very simple and demonstrates how you can create several different set-ups with just two pallets—see the photos overleaf. Have an L-shaped lounge sofa for lazy sunny afternoons, a long bench when a crowd comes by for a barbecue, or place them opposite each other when you want a catch up with a friend over a cup of tea. You don't have just one sofa—you have one for every occasion!

YOU WILL NEED:

Two pallets

Measuring rule

Pencil

Reciprocating saw or handsaw

Palm sander

Short furniture legs—mine are Brattvåg from Ikea

Drill driver with wood drill bit

Wood glue (optional)

4 nuts

Paint and paintbrush

Two mattresses—mine are child-sized ones, 24 x 48 inches (60 x 120cm)

1 No pallet is the same, so have a look at which way your pallet will work best as a sofa, to fit your mattress and to suit your outside space. Measure and mark where you need to cut the pallet to fit your mattress. Pallets are usually about 48 inches (120cm) long— I cut mine down to a width of 24 inches (60cm).

2 I used a reciprocating saw (see page 12) to cut my pallets, but you can use a handsaw too. Cut along the line you have drawn, through the entire depth of the sofa. Repeat to cut the second pallet to size.

3 Using a palm sander, sand your pallets smooth all over.

4 Attach the legs by drilling a hole the size of the leg thread in each corner on the underside of the pallet, 2 inches (5cm) in from the edge.

5 Push the leg through and secure in place with a nut. If your pallet is too thick for the thread of your furniture leg, apply wood glue to the top of the leg and glue in place (the thread should fit snugly in the wood).

6 Paint the pallets all over— I used Cuprinol Matt Wood Paint in Urban Slate. When dry, add your mattresses (mine are covered in fabric from Cloth & Candy, using similar colors but different patterns).

CHAPTER 2

PRETTY PRACTICAL

BIRDHOUSES

Why have just one birdhouse when you can have a whole village! These houses are all variations of the pink basic birdhouse. I deliberately used very rough pallet planks as I wanted lots of wonky areas to add character to these little builds. I used my birdhouses to frame the entrance to the farmhouse. The simple arch is made from three white-painted planks screwed together and drilled into the fence.

YOU WILL NEED:

Pallet wood planks

Measuring rule

Saw

Palm sander or sandpaper

Drill driver with ⅛-inch (2-mm) wood drill piece

Paddle drill bits, 1 inch (25mm) and 1¼ or 1½ inches (35 or 38mm)

Wood glue

1-inch (25-mm) nails and hammer

Paint and paintbrush

Black Sharpie (optional)

Matt outdoor varnish

Filler

Masking tape

Pencil

BASIC HOUSE

1 The pink birdhouse is the most basic of the four houses. It is one plank deep and two planks wide. Measure your plank width—mine is 3 inches (7.5cm)—and cut two pieces of 6 inches (15cm) for the sides, four pieces of 6¼ inches (16cm) for the front and back, and two pieces of 5½ inches (14cm) for the roof. Sand all the cut edges.

2 Lay out your birdhouse pieces—two pieces flat for the back, two sides, and topped with the two pieces for the front. For the base, measure the internal dimensions of your house and cut a plank to fit inside. Mine is 5 x 3 inches (12.5 x 7.5cm).

3 In one of the front planks, drill an entry hole using the paddle drill bit—the ideal entry hole is 1½ inches (38mm), but I only had a 1¼-inch (35-mm) paddle drill bit.

4 In the front and back planks, pre-drill the holes for the nails with the ⅛-inch (2-mm) drill bit, to prevent the wood splitting. You need three per side, ½ inch (1cm) in from the edges.

5 Apply wood glue to the short sides of the base and attach the side pieces. Apply more glue and stick the front and back pieces in place, then nail together through the pre-drilled holes.

6 Glue and nail the base in place, pre-drilling the nail holes and making sure the entry hole is in the upper part of the house. Glue and nail the roof in place, with the overhang above the entry hole.

7 Sand the birdhouse to smooth all the edges. Paint your house—I used Annie Sloan Chalk Paint® in Henrietta. When dry, add details in other paint colors or using a black Sharpie, then apply a matt outdoor varnish.

TALL TOWNHOUSE

8 Cut four 12-inch (30-cm) planks for the sides, front, and back, one 4½-inch (11-cm) plank for the base, one 4½-inch (11-cm) plank for the roof, and one 2 x 2¾-inch (5 x 7-cm) piece of plank for the middle floor. Screw the middle floor to the middle of the two sides.

9 Glue and nail together following the instructions for the basic house. The front piece has two slightly smaller entry holes of 1 inch (2.5cm) as this house will attract smaller birds.

10 If your wood is very wonky and you have large holes, you can fill them with filler before sanding and painting the house. I painted this house in Annie Sloan Chalk Paint® in Emile, with dots in Pure.

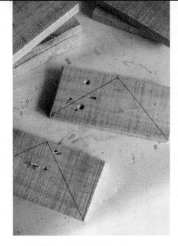

PITCHED ROOF HOUSE

11 You need two extra triangles for this house. Cut two 6-inch (15-cm) planks for the sides, six 6¼-inch (16-cm) planks for the front and back, three 4½-inch (11.5-cm) planks and one 4-inch (10-cm) plank for the roof, and one 5-inch (12.5-cm) plank for the base. To make the triangles, take two of the 6¼-inch (16-cm) side planks, mark the midpoint on one long side, and draw cutting lines to the corners.

12 Glue and nail together following the instructions for the basic house. However, you won't be able to nail the triangle to the other front piece so just use glue and hold in place with masking tape until the glue is dry. One roof slat is ⅝ inch (1.5cm) shorter—position this piece in line with the right angle of the triangle so you have an overlap at the apex of the roof. This means the overhang on the sides will be the same. I painted this house in Annie Sloan Chalk Paint® in Pure and Graphite.

MID-CENTURY HOUSE

13 For this house you need four 8-inch (20-cm) planks for the sides, front, and back, one 4 ⅜-inch (11-cm) plank for the base, and one 6-inch (15-cm) plank for the roof. Glue and nail together following the instructions for the basic house but with an asymmetric roof overhanging at one side, rather than at the front. I painted this house in Annie Sloan Chalk Paint® in Duck Egg Blue, with details added in Pure and Graphite.

OUTDOOR KITCHEN

I love my outdoor kitchen—for me, there is nothing better than having friends or family come over and serving them food outside. This kitchen has a tiled top for easy food prep, and also acts as a heatproof surface to stand my tabletop wood stove on. The large enamel basin acts as a little sink—use it to wash vegetables or fill it with ice cubes to keep your drinks cool. When you're done, just lift the basin out and tip the water away.

YOU WILL NEED:

Outdoor treated wood—2¾ x 1¾ inches (7 x 4.5cm) for the legs, and 1¾ x 1⅝ inches (4.5 x 4.2cm) for the frame

Pallet wood planks

Outdoor plywood, ¾ inch (18mm) thick

Tiles—mine are from Porcelain Superstore

Enamel basin, 14 inches (36cm) in diameter—mine is from Falcon

Measuring rule

Saw

Drill driver with wood drill bit and countersink bit

Wood screws

Filler

Palm sander or sandpaper

Paint and paintbrush

Nail gun or hammer and nails

Matt outdoor varnish

Wood glue

String and pencil

Jigsaw

Tile adhesive

Grout and spatula

1 Decide how large you want your kitchen top to be— lay your tiles out on a flat surface and place the large basin to the side, then measure the rectangle they make. Mine is three tiles deep and four tiles wide (I wanted to avoid cutting the tiles as their patterns are so pretty), plus enough space around the basin.

2 Cut the leg timber to make four legs of 29½ inches (75cm).

3 To make the frame, cut two longer lengths of 41¼ inches (105cm) for the front and back edges and two shorter lengths of 20 inches (50cm) for the sides. Screw the longer pieces to the top of the legs, pre-drilling and countersinking the screw holes first.

4 Screw the shorter side pieces to the table legs as well, making a rectangular frame with the legs attached inside the frame.

5 Stand the frame upright on its four legs. Now measure for the frame to support the lower shelf. Measure the inside measurement between the legs, along the sides and along the front and back. Cut the wood to these dimensions.

6 Measure 14 inches (35cm) down from the top frame and mark the drill hole on the inside of the table legs. Also make a mark at 13¼ inches (34cm) and another at 14¼ inches (36cm) on the front of the leg (the marks must be diagonal, as shown in the photo). Drill and countersink these holes.

7 Screw the inner frame to the legs, lining up the wood so it is flush with the outer sides of the legs.

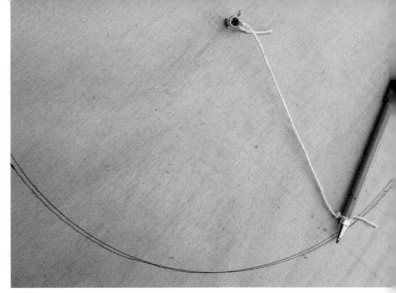

8 Fill the screw holes with filler. When it is dry, sand it smooth. Paint the entire frame white—I used Annie Sloan Chalk Paint® in Original. Let dry, then add a coat of matt outdoor varnish.

9 Measure the top of the frame and cut your plywood to fit—mine is 20 x 45 inches (50 x 114cm). Sand the cut side smooth. Glue and nail the plywood to the frame.

10 Cut out the gap for your basin. My bowl is 14 inches (36cm) in diameter, so I needed to cut a 13½-inch (35-cm) hole to allow the lip of the basin to rest on the wood. Find the middle of where the bowl will be and hammer in a nail or screw. Tie a pencil to a piece of string, then tie this to the nail at a length of 6¾ inches (17.5cm). Draw a circle with the pencil.

11 Drill a hole in the plywood to fit your jigsaw and cut the circle out. Sand the edges smooth, but be careful you don't make the opening any bigger. Paint the kitchen top the same color as the legs and let dry.

12 Following the instructions on your tub of tile adhesive, stick the tiles to the plywood and let set.

13 Cut the pallet planks for the shelf—mine are 15¾ inches (40cm) long. Sand smooth. Glue and nail the slats in place, leaving little gaps between the planks and spacing them equidistantly.

14 Grout the tiles according to the instructions on the packaging, wiping off any excess grout.

WOODEN DECKING

I love houses with a deck or verandah. There's something special about the wood framing the house—or, in my case, my workshop at the end of the garden. This is the perfect spot for a table and chair, for moments when I can take a quick break from work and relax with a coffee.

YOU CAN MAKE THE DECK AS LARGE AS YOU WISH. FOR EASE, THE DECK IN FRONT OF MY WORKSHOP IS THE DEPTH OF A PALLET PLANK.

YOU WILL NEED:

Outdoor treated wood, 1½ x 1½ inches (4 x 4cm)

Pallet wood planks (sand before using and only use thick, undamaged planks as the deck needs to be strong)

Measuring rule

Saw

Pencil

Drill driver with wood drill bit

Wood screws

Spirit level

Nail gun or hammer and nails

Jigsaw

Palm sander

1 Cut your treated wood to create a frame the size of your deck. You need long lengths of wood to lie parallel with your building, spaced 16 inches (40cm) apart. Shorter length spacer pieces of wood are placed between the parallel lines for strength—these are positioned at least every 20 inches (50cm). Space your frame out on the ground.

2 Mark where you need to drill holes for screws. Pre-drill the screw holes and screw the frame together. I did the first few joins on my work bench, then attached the other pieces to it on the ground.

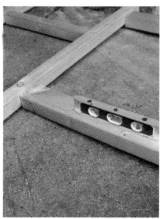

3 If you build your deck on grass or sand, you can level the ground before building. If, like me, you are building on concrete, use a spirit level to check your frame is level; if it isn't, prop it up with scrap pieces of wood.

4 Nail the sanded pallet planks to the frame, nailing each end to the outer frame and adding another row of nails to the long central strut of the frame.

5 Trim the planks level along the front edge of the deck using a jigsaw—it is easier to trim them after they have been attached to the frame rather than cutting them before you nail them in place. Sand any rough edges.

6 Add more sanded pallet planks to the front of the deck, to hide the framework.

GARDEN GAZEBO

The fabric canopy of this gazebo provides plenty of shade on a summer's day, but the structure also adds a charming element to evening gatherings. This gazebo is made one pallet plank deep, but you can make it a lot bigger simply by adding more support poles. If you would like to use the gazebo as a permanent structure in your garden, I suggest digging the legs into the soil. You can paint the gazebo any color you like, but I left mine natural for a rustic look.

YOU WILL NEED:

Pallet planks—I used 8 planks

4 fence posts, 3 x 3 inches (7.5 x 7.5cm) and 78 inches (2m) long

Measuring rule

Saw

Palm sander

Wood glue

Drill driver with wood drill bit

Wood screws

4 corner brackets

2 yards (2m) fabric— I used Neon Fleck by Cloth & Candy

Pins

Sewing machine

Sewing thread

2 dowels, each 59 inches (1.5m) long

1 Work out how big you want your gazebo to be—I like to lay the pallet wood for the horizontal beams on the ground to get a feel for the size. I went with 71 x 42½ inches (180 x 108cm)—the smaller measurement was chosen simply because this was my plank length. Cut the planks to size and sand smooth.

2 If you need to join planks together to make a longer length, glue and screw a 12-inch (30-cm) scrap piece of wood over the joint. Apply screws to both sides of the plank.

3 Screw one side length of pallet wood in between two fence posts.

4 Screw the front and back lengths of pallet wood to the fence posts too, creating your gazebo frame. Sand the fence posts smooth.

5 Make another long horizontal beam from pallet wood by gluing and screwing a scrap piece on the joint as in step 2. Screw in two corner brackets to each end.

6 Screw this plank across the middle of your gazebo structure. This will create a more stable structure and give you somewhere to hang the fabric canopy and to suspend lights from.

7 I used the full width of the fabric so there was no need to hem the long sides. To hem the shorter front and back ends, fold over the fabric by ½ inch (1cm) and stitch in place.

8 To form the front overhang of fabric and the casing for the dowel, at one end fold 12 inches (30cm) of fabric over, wrong sides facing, and stitch along the fold line. Stitch another line 4 inches (10cm) from the edge to make a tunnel for the dowel.

9 At the other end, fold the fabric double, 4 inches (10cm) from the end, creating a tunnel for the dowel, and stitch in place.

10 Cut your dowels to match the fabric width and insert into the tunnel stitched in the canopy. Hang the canopy over your gazebo with the right side facing down.

TO WORK OUT THE LENGTH OF FABRIC NEEDED FOR THE CANOPY, YOU NEED TO MEASURE THE LENGTH OF YOUR GAZEBO AND ADD 36 INCHES (1M). THE FABRIC WIDTH HAS TO BE AT LEAST 20 INCHES (50CM) NARROWER THAN THE WIDTH OF THE GAZEBO, SO YOU HAVE A GAP OF 10 INCHES (25CM) ON BOTH SIDES.

DOG BED

Your favorite canine needs a comfy spot in the garden too, and a pallet cut in half makes the perfect base for a dog bed. My little dog Kermit sure loves his new throne, which I painted a striking bright blue.

YOU WILL NEED:

Pallet

Dog bed mattress—mine is from Wilko

Measuring rule

Saw

Palm sander or sandpaper

Hammer and crowbar

Pencil

Drill driver with ¼-inch (4-mm) wood drill bit

1¾-inch (45-mm) wood screws

Wood glue

2 corner brackets

Masking tape (optional)

Paint and paintbrush

Matt outdoor varnish

1 First measure out the base of the bed. Place your dog mattress on the pallet and mark where you need to cut to fit your mattress best. This all depends on the size of your dog. My bed (for a medium-sized dog) measures 20½ x 31½ inches (52 x 80cm), which neatly fitted one side of the pallet and meant I could saw just to one side of the center strut.

2 To make the backrest, cut the remaining side of the pallet to the height of your pallet plus 10 inches (25cm)—for me, that is a total of 16 inches (40cm). Sand all the cut edges. Discard the middle bit of your pallet—use it for the side pieces or save it for another build.

3 The wooden blocks that form part of the pallet framework are not necessary on the backrest, so prise these off using a hammer and crowbar. (You can leave them if you wish, but they will make your bed heavier and bulkier.) Remove any nails left after removing the blocks. If necessary, reattach the slats to the frame.

4 Line up the backrest against the base and mark on the upright back slats where they meet. Using a ¼-inch (4-mm) drill bit, pre-drill holes ½ inch (1cm) below this line and screw together, from the back into the base.

5 Screw the bottom slats to the framework in the same way, but instead of marking where they meet just eyeball the pre-drilling.

6 To add the sides, measure the length the side rest needs to be—mine is 20 inches (51cm). Cut two pieces of pallet wood to this measurement and apply glue to the bottom. Screw the side pieces in place from the back of the bed, once again pre-drilling the holes first.

7 Screw a corner bracket halfway along each side piece for extra support. Sand the bed all over.

8 You can leave the bed as natural wood or paint it a bright color—I chose Annie Sloan Chalk Paint® in Greek Blue. I taped off the letter K (for Kermit) before painting, removing the tape right after painting for clean edges on this detail. When the paint is dry, add a coat of matt outdoor varnish.

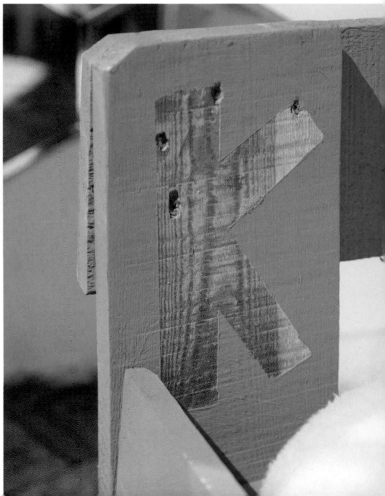

SLATTED FENCE

A fence built from thin wooden slats can provide privacy in your outside space, without completely blocking you off from the outside world, and this one also doubles up as a great spot from which to hang planters! I've planted mine with herbs, and their vibrant green leaves contrast well with the silver of the pots. The fence is also great for suspending bunting or pontoon lights.

THE DIMENSIONS OF THIS BUILD ARE COMPLETELY DEPENDENT ON WHAT KIND OF SPACE OR GARDEN YOU HAVE, SO YOU CAN ADJUST THE PROJECT TO SUIT YOUR OWN OUTSIDE SPACE. HERE THE FENCE RAISES THE HEIGHT OF MY GARDEN WALL, BUT YOU COULD ALSO USE THIS IDEA TO ADD A TRELLIS ABOVE AN EXISTING FENCE.

YOU WILL NEED:

Fence posts

Pallet wood planks, cut into 1½ -inch (4-cm) wide planks

Drill driver with wood drill bit and masonry drill bit

Pencil

Wall plugs

Wood screws long enough to go through the fence posts and into the wall

Saw

1¾-inch (40-mm) wood screws

Metal plant pots

Metal "S" hooks

1 Attach the fence posts to your existing wall by drilling a hole through the post at the bottom, middle, and top. Hold the first fence post against the wall and mark where the holes are, then drill a corresponding hole in the wall. Insert a wall plug and screw the fence post to the wall.

2 The distance between fence posts depends on the length of your pallet planks. My planks are 60 inches (1.5m) long, so I have a post every 58 inches (1.45m) to allow 2 inches (5cm) of each plank to overlap the post. Screw the pallet planks horizontally to the fence posts.

3 Drill a hole in the metal plant pots just below the top lip, then attach an "S" hook and hang from the slats. If you wish, you can also drill a drainage hole in the base of the metal plant pot.

PLAY TENT

Turn your pallet wood into a play tent for your child or dog! Made from salvaged wood, this tent will look great as a permanent structure on your lawn. I don't now what your pet is like, but my dog Kermit loves to snuggle up, so this tent and a soft blanket make the perfect snooze spot for him. For children, the tent is a great spot for tea parties, "secret society" hideaways, or just a spot to read a book. My baby Kiki is a little small for all this make-believe, but she sure likes it as chill spot. To shelter your child from the sun, drape fabric over the wooden structure to create some shade.

YOU WILL NEED:

2 pieces of 1½ x ¾-inch (4 x 2-cm) white wood, each 63 inches (160cm) long

Pallet wood—I used planks 3 inches (7.5cm) wide

Measuring rule

Miter saw or handsaw with miter box

Palm sander or sandpaper

Clamp

Drill driver with ¼-inch (5-mm) and ½-inch (12-mm) wood drill bits

Wooden dowel, ½ inch (12mm) thick, 18 inches (45cm) long

Pencil

Chisel

Hammer

Wood screws

> MY TENT IS THE PERFECT SIZE FOR BABIES AND SMALL DOGS, WITH A POLE LENGTH OF 31½ INCHES (80CM). FOR TODDLERS AND BIGGER DOGS, MAKE THE SIDES 43 INCHES (110CM) LONG.

1 To make the frame, cut each length of white wood into two pieces 31½ inches (80cm) long and sand smooth. Clamp the four pieces together and drill a ¼-inch (4-mm) pilot hole 1¼ inches (3cm) down from one end. With the pieces still clamped together, change to the ½-inch (12-mm) drill bit and drill a bigger hole. Sand smooth.

2 Push the dowel through the drilled holes.

3 Ease the pieces of wood along the dowel so that there are two at each end of the dowel. Position them 2 inches (5cm) in from the ends of the dowel and open them out at a 45-degree angle. At one end, mark where the two pieces overlap.

4 Remove the marked piece of wood from the dowel and chisel out the overlap to half the depth of the wood. To do this, make several cuts with your saw to half the depth of the wood, then use a hammer and chisel to carve out the wood. Slot the pieces together back on the dowel.

5 Using the miter saw, cut the pallet wood pieces to fill the triangular end of the frame. The measurements depend on the width of the planks you use and the space you leave between them. For my 3-inch (7.5-cm) wide planks, I cut planks to 24, 20½, 17, 12½, 8¾, and 5 inches (60, 52, 43, 32, 22, and 13cm). Remember that each plank will overhang the frame by the width of the wood used for the side slats. Cut both ends of each plank at a 20-degree angle.

6 Sand the planks smooth so there are no rough edges anywhere—this is especially important to avoid babies or young children getting splinters or scratches.

7 Screw the planks in place to form the triangular end. Make sure you have an overlap on both sides the thickness of the pallet wood—I use a little offcut of wood to ensure the overhang is a consistent size throughout.

8 Measure the sides to see how long you need to cut the wood. Remember that the side slats need to line up with the end-piece slats. For my tent, the side pieces measured 19, 18½, 17½, 17, 16¼, 16 inches (47, 46, 44.5, 43, 41.5, and 41cm). Cut these measurements twice, to fill both sides. Sand the planks smooth.

9 Screw the side pieces in place, making sure the slats line up with the slats on the triangular end and butting the ends together. For a flush finish, sand any corners that don't quite overlap.

10 To make the front, measure how long the two pieces of wood need to be. For my tent, they measured 6 and 9 inches (15 and 23cm). As in step 5, cut the ends of these planks at a 20-degree angle. Sand and screw in place.

GARDEN TRUG

A traditional wooden trug is the perfect vessel to carry around the garden when you pick your home-grown flowers, fruits, and vegetables. But who am I kidding? I can't grow a vegetable to save my life, so I'll just use mine for displaying pretty plants and trinkets!

YOU WILL NEED:

Pallet wood planks—
I used 3

Measuring rule

Pencil

Saw

Palm sander or sandpaper

Wood glue

Nail gun or hammer
and nails

Drill driver with ³⁄₈-inch
(9-mm) wood drill bit

Four 1-inch (25-mm) wood
screws

Wooden dowel, ³⁄₈ inch
(9mm) in diameter

Wood stain and
lint-free cloth

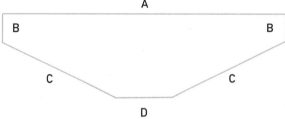

A = 14½ inches (36.75cm)
B = half plank width, 1½ inches (3.75cm)
C = two plank widths, 6 inches (15cm)
D = one plank width, 3 inches (7.5cm)

1 The trug shape is dependent on the width of your plank. My planks are 3 inches (7.5cm) wide, so my measurements are as per the diagram above. The sides (B) are half a plank wide, the bottom sides (C) are two planks wide, and the base (D) is one plank wide.

2 Measure out and draw one trug side on a pallet wood plank. Cut this out, and then draw around it on another plank to make the second side. Sand smooth.

3 For the trug base, cut six planks 10 inches (25cm) long. Cut one of these planks in half widthwise. Sand smooth.

4 Glue and then nail the five full-width planks to the sides of your trug. Start with one plank on the flat base, then attach two planks to either side.

5 Glue and nail the half-width planks to the two ends of the trug.

6 To make the handle uprights, cut an 8¾-inch (22-cm) length of pallet plank, then cut in half widthwise to make two narrow pieces. Sand smooth. Drill a ⅜-inch (9-mm) hole in each piece of wood, ¾ inch (2cm) down from the top.

7 Glue and then screw the handles to the inside of the trug, making sure they are exactly opposite each other and the drilled holes are at the top.

8 Cut the dowel to 10 inches (25cm) and push through the holes. It should be a snug fit, but you can add a dab of glue to secure it in place if you wish.

9 Add a coat of wood stain to the trug, or you can paint it any color you like.

STORAGE HOUSE

If you have a fireplace or firepit, you'll need somewhere to stack your logs and this little storage house is ideal. The shelf is great for keeping other garden paraphernalia like pots, twine, and scissors close at hand, too. The tall, narrow shape makes me think of the canal houses back home in Holland, so the shelf is the perfect place to display my daughter's tiny clogs! If you don't have to store logs (or clogs!), but would like more garden storage space, you can add extra shelves.

YOU WILL NEED:

Planed smooth batten, 1³⁄₈ x 1³⁄₈ inches (34 x 34mm)

Pallet wood planks

Measuring rule

Saw

Paint and paintbrush

Wood glue

Miter saw or handsaw and miter box

Nail gun or hammer and nails

Clamps (optional)

Little doorknobs or hooks (optional)

Palm sander

Outdoor varnish

I MADE MY HOUSE FOUR PLANKS DEEP, USING 6¾-INCH (17.5-CM) WIDE PLANKS WITH A THICKNESS OF ¾ INCH (1.5CM). YOU CAN EASILY ADJUST THE DIMENSIONS OF THE HOUSE TO SUIT YOUR PALLET WOOD.

1 The planed smooth batten forms the four corner supports in the main part of the house. Cut four pieces of this timber to the depth of the house—for me, that's 12¼ inches (31cm). Paint them and let dry— I used Annie Sloan Chalk Paint® in Henrietta.

2 Cut the shelf of your house— four pallet planks of 17¼ inches (44cm) and one piece of 12¼ inches (31cm) as the central support. Glue the sides of the planks together and keep in place by nailing the central support across the middle. Paint the shelf too.

3 Cut eight pallet planks for the two tall sides of the house, each 41¾ inches (106cm) tall. The bottom has a straight cut, but the top is cut using a miter saw (or handsaw and miter box) on a 15-degree angle.

4 You also need to cut four pallet planks for the base, each 18½ inches (47cm) long (ie 17¼ inches /44cm plus the thickness of the wood) and cut with straight ends.

5 Line up four long planks side by side. Place a painted piece of batten across the bottom, lined up with the ends of the planks, and glue and nail in place.

6 Glue and nail another piece of painted batten to the top, ¾ inch (1.5cm) from the top edge (this is the edge with the 15-degree angle).

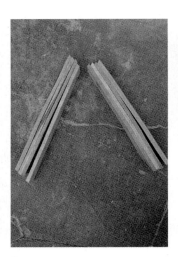

7 Glue and nail the base planks to the batten (I used my workbench to keep the planks in place). Then make up the second side of the house and attach that to the base in the same way.

8 Glue and nail the shelf to the top of the house, making sure that the central support faces into the house. I used my nail gun, but you can use a hammer and nails if you wish.

9 Now cut the roof planks. You need eight planks 18½ inches (47cm) long, with one end cut to 15 degree (bottom) and the other end cut to 30 degree (top)—this will allow the sloping sides of the roof to butt up neatly.

10 Apply glue to both ends of the roof planks and to the top of the house sides. Place the first pair of roof planks in place, making sure they meet centrally. Carefully nail the base of the roof planks to the sides of the house, and then nail the roof planks together where they meet at the apex of the roof.

11 Apply glue to the sides of the first roof plank and place the second plank against it (it may help to keep it in place with clamps while the glue sets). Nail in place on the sides and in the top joint. Continue until all four pairs of planks are in place. (I found it easiest to add one row at a time and let the glue set with clamps before gluing and nailing in the next pair.)

12 Cut the pallet planks to cover the back of the house. Measure the width and cut enough planks to fill in from the base to the shelf (my top plank extended up a little behind the shelf). Glue and nail in place.

13 If you wish, add little knobs or hooks inside the house, handy for hanging scissors and gardening equipment.

14 Sand the house, running your sander over the joints a couple of times to make them nice and smooth. Varnish.

CHAPTER 3
PALLET PLANTERS

GARDEN SCREEN

This simple project is the ideal way to screen off an area of the garden or to add a touch of privacy to a deck or patio. The easy-to-make plant boxes are supported by a simple frame and planted with a wide variety of flowers to give you lots of color and fragrance.

I MADE MY FRAME TO SLOT BETWEEN TWO PILLARS AT THE EDGE OF A VERANDAH, BUT YOU CAN ADJUST THE DIMENSIONS TO SUIT YOUR OWN SPACE.

MY PLANTERS ARE A VARIETY OF STYLES AND SIZES—SOME HAVE FOUR SIDES OF THE SAME HEIGHT, WHILE OTHERS HAVE STAGGERED HEIGHTS. THE LENGTH OF THE PLANTERS WILL DEPEND ON HOW WIDELY SPACED YOUR FRAME UPRIGHTS ARE, BUT REMEMBER THAT LONG PLANTERS WILL NEED TO BE ATTACHED TO THE FRAME IN SEVERAL PLACES, TO SUPPORT THE WEIGHT.

THE SCREEN LOOKS BEST WITH AT LEAST THREE LONG PLANTERS. IF YOU WISH, YOU CAN ADD DRAINAGE HOLES TO THE BASE OF THE PLANTERS. I ALSO USED A TINY OFFCUT OF PALLET WOOD AS AS SHELF FOR A SMALL PLANT POT.

YOU WILL NEED:

Pallet planks of the same width

White wood for the frame, 1⅞ x 3 inches (47 x 75mm)—I used 5 lengths each of 94 inches (2.4m)

Measuring rule

Saw

Palm sander or sandpaper

Wood glue

Nail gun or nails and a hammer

Corner brackets (optional)

Drill driver with wood drill bit

Wood screws

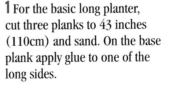

1 For the basic long planter, cut three planks to 43 inches (110cm) and sand. On the base plank apply glue to one of the long sides.

2 Place another plank against it and nail together. I used my nail gun, but you can use a hammer and nails if you wish. Apply the other plank in the same way on the other side.

3 Measure the size your sides need to be—this should be the width of your pallet plank plus twice the width. For me, it's 4 inches (10cm). Cut the sides and sand.

4 Glue and nail the sides to the planter. Add some drainage holes to the base of the planter.

5 To create some variation to your screen, make planters where the fronts are glued and nailed on top of the base plank. The sides are made a bit taller but are still the same width as the base plank.

6 Alternatively, glue and nail the front in front of the base plank and the back on top to create a height difference. You can then have sides that are not flush.

7 Or, as seen here, emphasize the height difference by giving the sides a soft slant.

8 To make the frame, screw two white-painted planks to your pillars or wall (make sure the tops of the planks are at the same height). Cut another plank to the correct length to fit between these two uprights and screw in place (if this is tricky, you could use corner brackets as well). The two remaining lengths of white wood are cut to the correct height and placed equidistantly between the pillars, then screwed in place. Screw the planters to your frame from the back using wood screws.

EASY PALLET PLANTER

If you are after a super-easy project, this is the planter for you. You don't even have to take the pallet apart— just chop it in half and you will have this done in under an hour! As the planter is so basic, I planted it with an abundance of color, perfect for brightening up an unloved corner of your garden.

YOU WILL NEED:

Pallet

Some spare pieces of wood for the planter bases (or use the other half of the pallet)

Measuring rule

Pencil

Saw

Drill drivern with wood drill bit

Wood screws

Hammer and crowbar

Palm sander or sandpaper

1 Mark your cutting lines and cut your pallet in half, sawing to one side of the central strut parallel to the vertical back slats.

2 Trim the original outer side of the planter if necessary, cutting off any overhanging wood to make it flush to the block of wood between the slats.

Easy Pallet Planter **87**

3 Stand the pallet the right way up, with the back slats vertical. Measure the space between the front and back of the pallet to work out the size of the piece of wood needed for the base of the top planter box. Cut a piece of pallet wood (from the discarded half of the pallet) to this size. If necessary, drill a couple of drainage holes.

4 Attach the base in place, screwing through the wooden slats, pre-drilling the holes first to prevent the slats from splitting. Create the middle planter box in the same way.

5 The bottom of the pallet has a bigger planter box, so you have to take off the front piece of wood. Use a hammer and crowbar, but keep the piece of wood you removed.

6 For the sides of the bottom planter box, cut 10-inch (25-cm) lengths of pallet wood (you can use the other half of the pallet for this). Screw these to the sides of the wooden blocks at the base of the planter. Screw the original front piece back in place on the new longer sides.

7 Measure the base and cut pallet planks to close it off— I needed three planks of 24 inches (60cm). If there are no gaps between the slats, drill some drainage holes.

8 Sand the whole planter smooth, then plant with your favorite flowers.

PRODUCE PLANTER

Give your home-grown vegetables their own special home with this produce planter. It's handy to position this just outside your kitchen door so you can harvest your herbs, salad leaves, or tomatoes as you are about to cook. With its tall legs and hand-painted decoration, this planter is sure to brighten up your garden.

YOU WILL NEED:

Pallet planks—I used 13 planks

Outdoor wood, 1¾ x 1½ inches (45 x 40mm)

Measuring rule

Saw

Drill driver with ⅛-inch (2-mm) wood drill bit

1 and 1¾-inch (24 and 44-mm) wood screws

Wood glue (optional)

Palm sander or sandpaper

Paint and paintbrush

Pencil

Black Sharpie

Matt outdoor varnish

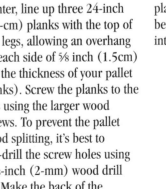

1 Cut your pallet planks, making sure they are all the same width:

- Six 24-inch (60-cm) lengths for the front and back

- Six 10½-inch (27-cm) lengths for the sides

- Four 24-inch (60-cm) lengths for the base

If your planks are wider or narrower, adjust the side length. The sides need to be four times the width of one plank minus twice the thickness of the planks.

2 To make the legs, cut the outdoor wood into four pieces of 31½ inches (80cm).

3 To make the front of the planter, line up three 24-inch (60-cm) planks with the top of two legs, allowing an overhang on each side of ⅝ inch (1.5cm) (or the thickness of your pallet planks). Screw the planks to the legs using the larger wood screws. To prevent the pallet wood splitting, it's best to pre-drill the screw holes using a ⅛-inch (2-mm) wood drill bit. Make the back of the planter in the same way.

4 To add the two sides of the planter, position the side planks between the legs and screw into place.

5 To add the base of the planter, attach the remaining four long planks using the shorter wood screws. The two outer planks will need to have a square cut out at each end to accommodate the legs.

6 To neaten the underside of the planter, I glued a few small offcuts of wood to the base around the legs to complete the edges. Sand any rough edges.

7 Paint the planter—I used Annie Sloan Chalk Paint® in Paris Grey. Let dry. If you wish, drill a couple of drainage holes in the base.

8 When the paint is dry, draw on your vegetable and flower shapes with a pencil, then paint them white.

9 When the white paint is dry, use a black Sharpie to add detail to your drawings. Give the planter a coat of outdoor matt varnish and let dry.

PLANTER BENCH

The perfect place to relax in a corner of your garden and catch the last of the sun's rays with a cold drink and a good book, this bench has a built-in planter and the grass will give a great rustling sound, the perfect soundtrack for a relaxing moment. I left my plants in pots, but you could plant straight into the planter if you drill a few drainage holes in the base. A great idea for a garden party would be to put little glass vases of flowers in the back, or even a rectangular container full of ice to keep your drinks cool at your next barbecue! If your bench is placed against a wall, you don't need to fill the back of the bench with wood.

YOU WILL NEED:

3 pieces of 1½ x ¾-inch (4 x 2-cm) white wood, each 94 inches (240cm) long

Pallet wood planks

Measuring rule

Saw

Drill driver with ¼-inch (4-mm) wood drill bit

Wood screws

Pencil

Clamp (optional)

Corner bracket

Palm sander

1 First make the two stands from the white wood. Cut the following:

• Two 31½-inch (80-cm) lengths, for the rear vertical piece

• Four 17½-inch (44-cm) lengths, for the base and seat horizontal pieces

• Two 16½-inch (42-cm) lengths, for the slanted back pieces

• Two 14¼-inch (36-cm) lengths, for the front vertical pieces

• Two 4¾-inch (12-cm) lengths, for the slanted back supports

2 Screw a 14¼-inch (36-cm) piece between two 17½-inch (44-cm) pieces and attach the 31½-inch (80-cm) piece to the open side, creating a shape that looks like the letter "d." Pre-drill all the holes to prevent the wood splitting when screwed together.

3 Screw a 4¾-inch (12-cm) piece to the long stand, 5½ inches (14cm) down from the top. Once again, pre-drill the hole first.

4 Lean another 16½-inch (42-cm) piece against the short ¾-inch (12-cm) piece, 9½ inches (24cm) in from the front edge of the seat support, and mark where it touches the short piece and the seat support. In the middle of these marks pre-drill a screw hole. Screw in the slanted piece to finish your stand. Repeat steps 2–4 to make another stand.

5 Decide on the length of the seat. I made mine 27½ inches (70cm)—if you go over 39 inches (100cm) you will need to add a third stand to support the seat planks. Cut your planks to the required length—the number of planks you need depends on how wide your pallet wood is (I used 13 planks for the front, seat, back, and planter).

6 Start screwing in pallet wood planks to form the seat. You want an overhang the depth of a plank at both ends—I used an offcut held up against the frame to get the right length. The front plank needs to have the same overhang too.

7 Next to be fitted are the planks on the front, which are also 27½ inches (70cm). Screw the top and bottom planks in place first, then space out the other ones evenly. Remember to give the sides an overhang the depth of a plank on both sides.

8 Attach the planks that cover the slanted backrest in the same way.

9 Measure for the sides of the bench. Start with the rectangular lower half and cut your planks to the right length. The length should be 18½ inches (47cm), as only the back needs to have an overhang here. Screw in place.

10 Measure the individual planks for the upper half of the side pieces—these will all have different lengths. Cut one end at a 15-degree angle. Make sure the back has the overhang— I clamped an offcut to the frame to give me the right measurements.

11 Now add the base of the planter. Cut a plank to 6⅛ x 22¾ inches (15.5 x 57.5cm) and attach in place with a corner bracket in the middle of the planter. The back will be held in place by the back panels. If you are going to pot plants directly into the planter, drill a few drainage holes in the plank.

12 Measure the back of the bench—you will not have any overhang here, so it should be around 26 inches (66cm). Cut your planks and screw them in place.

13 To attach the base of the planter to the back, pre-drill a few holes and screw the back plank to the base of the planter. If your seat will be against a wall, you don't need to fill the back up with planks—just the planter back will do. If your seat is freestanding, fill the rest of the back down to the base.

14 With all the wood in place, use a palm sander to smooth the edges and give the planks a final sand. You can paint the seat any color you fancy or just keep it natural, as I've done.

HEXAGONAL PLANTER

Not all planters need to be round or square—try building a hexagon instead! I filled my hexagon with small vases and displayed a bouquet of peonies and roses—the pink petals look so good against the textured white wood. You could also grow your favorite herbs in the planter and hang it in your kitchen as a handy chef's mini garden. Either display the planter on a table, as shown here, or hang it on the wall (you'll need to knock two nails into the wall to suspend it from).

YOU WILL NEED:

Pallet wood

Measuring rule

Miter saw or handsaw with miter box

Palm sander or sandpaper

Wood glue

Masking tape

Drill driver with $\frac{1}{16}$-inch (2-mm) wood drill bit

1½-inch (40-mm) nails

Hammer

Pencil

Paint and paintbrush

1 To make the outer frame, cut six pieces of pallet wood, each 12 inches (30cm) long, with the ends cut at a 30-degree angle (the angled ends point toward each other—refer to the photo). Sand the pieces smooth.

2 Lay your pieces of wood on a flat surface in a hexagon shape, butting the ends together—this will ensure that you line up the angled ends in the right direction. Apply wood glue to two of the angled ends and press them together. Repeat with the remaining ends to form a glued-together hexagon.

3 Carefully wrap masking tape around your hexagon so all pieces stay in place during the drying process. Leave on a flat surface and let dry (check the drying time specified by the glue manufacturer).

4 When the glue is dry and the hexagon feels secure, pre-drill three holes in each joint, ½ inch (1cm) in from the short end—two holes in one piece ¾ inch (2cm) from the top and bottom edges and one hole in the other end halfway between the other holes. Nail the pieces together using the pre-drilled holes.

5 To make the back panel, place two or three pieces of pallet wood (depending on width) on top of the hexagon, lining them up with the hexagon base. Draw a cutting line on each piece. Do the same on the back of the hexagon frame, using one additional plank so the back is higher. Cut and sand the wood.

6 Glue the back panel in place, then pre-drill holes and nail the planks in place. Attach the front panel in the same way.

7 Sand the hexagon frame and front and back panels smooth.

8 Give the finished planter a lick of paint, using any color you like (I used Annie Sloan Chalk Paint® in Original), and let dry.

LETTER PLANTER

This is the perfect planter if you are not so good at keeping plants alive! Filled to the brim with the most beautiful artificial flowers, it's also a great way to have colorful flowers on display all year.

TURNING YOUR INITIAL INTO A PLANTER WORKS FOR ALMOST EVERY LETTER, BUT IS A LITTLE TRICKIER IF IT'S A ROUNDED LETTER. IF THAT'S THE CASE, SEARCH FOR DIFFERENT TYPEFACES ONLINE TO FIND A SIMPLER SHAPE. LUCKILY FOR ME, MY INITIAL IS MADE UP OF STRAIGHT LINES!

YOU WILL NEED:

Plywood, ½ inch (10mm) or thicker

Pallet wood planks

Measuring rule

Pencil

Jigsaw

Palm sander or sandpaper

Glue gun

Hammer and nails

Artificial flowers—mine are from Ikea and Hobbycraft

1 On your plywood draw a rectangle measuring 14 x 12 inches (35 x 30cm). Draw your letter within this rectangle, making sure all the edges are straight.

2 Cut your letter out using a jigsaw. I've found the best way to cut the sharp corners is to cut a soft curve first and then go back and cut out the corner. Sand the cut edges smooth.

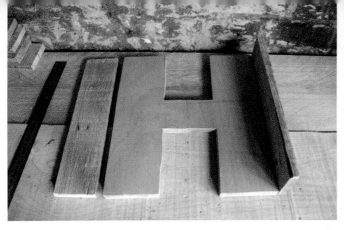

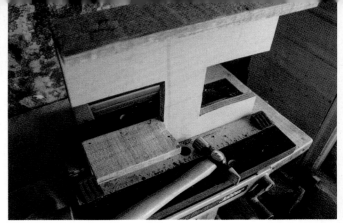

3 Line your pallet planks up along the outside of your letter and mark where you need to cut them. Do the same with the inside edges of your letter. Cut the planks and sand them smooth.

4 Glue and then nail the planks to the plywood base.

5 Measure and then cut smaller pieces of pallet wood to fill in the gaps. Glue and nail them in place. Sand any rough edges smooth.

6 Cut the stems off the artificial flowers and arrange the flowers inside the letter. I put more flowers in the top left and bottom right corners for a flowing effect, but you can fill the whole planter as full as you wish or only use a few blooms. Glue them in place when you are happy with the arrangement.

7 To protect your fingers from burning on the hot glue, use a little stick (like this plant marker) to push the flower into the glue.

HANGING PLANTER

If space is limited on your terrace or balcony, why not make this hanging planter? You can hang it from a hook on your wall or fence, and a couple displayed together make a great vertical garden feature.

YOU WILL NEED:

Pallet wood planks, all the same width and sanded smooth

Batten, ¾ x ¾ inch (2 x 2cm)

Measuring rule

Saw

Wood glue

Nail gun or hammer and nails

Drill driver

Bowl

Pencil

Palm sander or sandpaper

Leather belt

Scissors

Two ¾-inch (20-mm) wood screws

Two washers

1 Cut your pallet wood planks to four lengths of 5⅛ inches (13cm) and eight lengths of 6 inches (15cm). Cut four pieces of batten which are 6 inches (15cm) less twice the thickness of the pallet wood. My wood is ⅝ inch (1.5cm) thick, so this makes it 6 - [2 x ⅝] = 4¾ inches (or 15 - [2 x 1.5] = 12cm).

2 Lay out the wood for the box—the front, back, and base use the longer pieces of wood and the sides use the shorter pieces. The battens hold it all together.

3 Glue and nail a piece of batten to two shorter planks, leaving an even space at the top and bottom for the lid and base. Make the other side in the same way.

4 Glue and nail the longer pieces to the batten too, continuing until all sides and the base are in place. If you wish, drill a drainage hole in the base.

5 Place the two remaining 6-inch (15-cm) pieces side by side. Place a bowl on top and trace around it to mark a circular opening (the bowl needs to be slightly smaller than the wood to allow a margin of about ¾ inch/2cm all around).

6 Cut out the circle and sand the wood smooth.

7 Glue and nail the circular lid to the battens and sides of the planter.

8 Cut off the buckle end of the leather belt, to leave a length of around 27½ inches (70cm). Shape the cut end to match the other end.

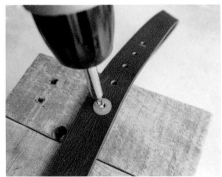

9 Push a washer around a screw and screw the belt to the planter. You can use one of the belt holes or just drill straight through the leather.

PLANT STANDS

I love these plant stands! They are so simple to build from a few pieces of scrap pallet wood and some short lengths of copper pipe, and you can make them in whatever size you like. Use them to showcase pots of your favorite flowers or plants on your terrace or patio. Alternatively, the stands come in very useful at barbecues—put knives and forks, napkins, and ice cubes in pots placed on the plant stands and you get a nice height difference on your serving station.

YOU WILL NEED:

Pallet plank

Strip wood, ¾ x ¼ inch (18 x 6mm)

Measuring rule

Saw

Palm sander or sandpaper

Wood glue

Drill driver with wood drill bit

⅝-inch (15-mm) wood screws

Sharpie

⅝-inch (15-mm) copper pipe, two 39-inch (1-m) pieces

Pipe cutter

Strong glue—I use Gorilla Glue

Four ⅝-inch (15-mm) copper equal tees

Four copper saddle clips

Eight ⅝-inch (15-mm) copper end caps

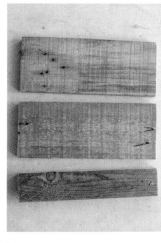

1 Cut the planks into three 7-inch (18-cm) lengths, then cut one plank in half widthwise. Sand smooth.

2 Cut a 7-inch (18-cm) piece of strip wood. Lay the pieces of pallet wood together with the half-width in the center. Apply wood glue to the long side of the planks and glue them together. Pre-drill three equidistant holes in the piece of strip wood and screw in place across the middle of the pallet wood, for extra strength.

3 Mark your pipes where you need to cut them with a Sharpie. You will need four lengths of 12 inches (30cm) for the legs and two lengths which are the combined width of the planks plus ¾ inch (2cm) — for me, that's 8¼ inches (21cm). Push the pipe into the pipe cutter, lining up the Sharpie mark with the blade and twist the cutter around until the cut has been made.

4 On each of the 12-inch (30-cm) legs, cut off a 2-inch (5-cm) length. Glue an equal tee between the 2-inch (5-cm) and 10-inch (25-cm) pieces.

5 Make two pairs of legs by gluing the 8¼-inch (21-cm) lengths of pipe into the equal tees. Let the glue dry.

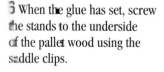

6 When the glue has set, screw the stands to the underside of the pallet wood using the saddle clips.

7 Using the strong glue, glue the end caps onto the pipes. If you have accidentally cut one of the pipes a little too short, you can even them out now by putting a bit of cardboard or tissue in the end cap before gluing.

8 I made the second plant stand a bit shorter with 6-inch (15-cm) legs. For this, cut your copper pipe into four lengths of 6 inches (15cm) and lengths of 7½ inches (19cm).

PLANTER WITH CONTRAST LEGS

This is another basic box planter given a design twist by having loose legs painted in a contrasting color. On its own, the box is super-useful around the house as a storage box for garden equipment, toys, or pillows, but sit it on little legs and this box will look great as a planter on your terrace. I painted the legs black to offset the light pallet wood, but a bright color would also look great.

YOU WILL NEED:

Pallet wood planks—I used 9 planks, all the same width

Batten 1⅓ x 1⅓ inches (34 x 34mm), 2 lengths of 71 inches (1.8m)

Measuring rule

Saw

Palm sander or sandpaper

Wood glue

Drill driver with wood drill bit and countersink bit

1½-inch (40-mm) wood screws

Clamps

Filler

Paint and paintbrush

Matt outdoor varnish

1 For the box, cut the pallet wood planks as follows:

• Six 24-inch (60-cm) plus twice the thickness of the wood (for me, that's 1¼ inches/3cm) lengths, for the front and back

• Six 9¼-inch (23.5-cm) lengths, for the sides

• Three 24-inch (60-cm) lengths, for the base

• From the batten, cut four pieces which are 3 x plank width—for me, that's 8½ inches (21.5cm)—for the vertical corner supports. Sand all the wood smooth.

2 On the front plank, line up two pieces of batten ⅝ inch (1.5cm) (or your pallet wood thickness) from the sides, flush with the top. Glue and screw in place, clamp, then attach the other two pallet planks to complete the front panel. At the bottom of the panel, the batten will fall short.

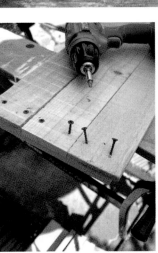

3 Glue and screw the other three long planks to the remaining batten to make the back panel.

4 Glue and screw the shorter side planks to the battens.

5 Attach the remaining panel to the sides, creating an open box. Make sure that the corner battens all fall short on the same side, or the box base will not sit evenly.

6 To make the base, cut two scrap pieces of pallet wood 8 inches (20cm) long. Glue and screw these to the base planks, 4 inches (10cm) from the short ends, creating another panel.

7 Drop the base into the box (where the battens fall short), then glue and screw in place. If the base slats don't have much space between them, drill some drainage holes.

8 To make the legs, check the width of your box—it should be 10½ inches (27cm). From the batten, cut two 10½-inch (27-cm) pieces and four 8-inch (20-cm) pieces.

9 Pre-drill and countersink a hole in all four shorter pieces, 3 inches (7.5cm) from the top.

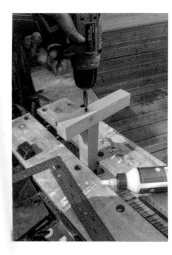

10 Glue and screw two short pieces to a long piece, creating a stretched-out H-shape. Repeat with the other leg, then fill in the screw holes with filler.

11 When the filler is dry, sand smooth and paint with your chosen color—I used Annie Sloan Chalk Paint® in Graphite. Let dry, then apply a coat of matt outdoor varnish. Sit the planter on the legs (these are not attached to the planter).

COPPER PLANTER

Once you know how to construct a basic box from pallet wood, you can build a whole array of different planters. Here I swapped the wooden legs for copper pipes, and I love how they stand out against the dark gray-painted wood. This planter would look great in a minimalistic garden or terrace.

YOU WILL NEED:

Sanded pallet wood planks, all the same width—mine are 3 inches (7.5cm)

White wood, ¾ x ⅝ inch (2 x 1.5cm), 48 inches (1.2m)

Wood trim, ¾ inch (2cm) wide, 48 inches (1.2m)

Measuring rule

Saw

Drill driver and wood drill bit

1-inch (25-mm) wood screws

Hammer and nails

Paint and paintbrush

Sharpie

⅝-inch (15-mm) copper pipe, two 39-inch (1-m) pieces

Pipe cutter

Eight ⅝-inch (15-mm) copper end caps

⅝-inch (15-mm) copper-colored wood screws

12 copper saddle clips

Wood glue

Strong glue—I use Gorilla Glue

1 Cut the pallet wood planks as follows:

• Eight 15¾-inch (40-cm) lengths, for the front and back

• Eight 7¾-inch (19.5-cm) lengths, for the sides

• Three 15¾-inch (40-cm) lengths, for the base

• From the white wood, cut four pieces which are 4 x plank width—for me, that's 12 inches (30cm)—for the vertical corner supports.

2 Line up four of the side planks next to each other. Screw in the white wood along the outer edges, pre-drilling the screw holes to prevent the wood splitting. Do the same with the other four short planks.

3 Line four of the longer planks up and screw the sides panels to them.

4 Do the same with another four planks to complete the box.

5 Screw the remaining four long planks on the base of the box. If there are no slits between the base planks, drill a few holes for drainage.

6 Cut your wood trim to the width and depth of your planter—mine is two lengths of 15¾ inches (40cm) and two of 7¾ inches (19.5cm). Nail it to the top of the planter, with the overhang on the outer side of the planter. The trim stops the copper legs from sliding up due to the weight of the plants and potting compost in the planter.

7 Paint the planter—I used Cuprinol Matt Wood Paint in Urban Slate (to match my Pallet Sofas on page 49).

8 To make the legs, measure and use a Sharpie to mark your pipes where you need to cut them—this planter has legs 20 inches (50cm) long. Use a copper pipe cutter to cut the pipes—push the pipe into the pipe cutter, lining up the Sharpie mark with the blade, and twist the cutter around until the cut has been made.

9 Using the strong glue, glue the end caps onto the pipes. If you have accidentally cut one of the pipes a little too short, you can even them out now by putting a bit of cardboard or tissue in the end cap before gluing.

10 Screw the legs onto the planter just below the trim, using three saddle clips on each leg.

CHAPTER 4

DECORATIVE ITEMS

OUTDOOR ART

Why limit yourself to hanging paintings only in the living room? Outdoor art can really enhance your terrace and outdoor spaces. You can even adapt the piece to include your family name and house number, and hang it by your front door. I used up little offcuts of pallet wood to make the succulents in this piece, but you can draw any plant, shape, or animal you like.

YOU WILL NEED:

5 pallet planks, each
16 inches (40cm) long

2 pieces of strip wood—
mine were ½ x 10 inches
(1 x 25cm)

Scrap pieces of pallet wood

Measuring rule

Saw

Palm sander or sandpaper

Drill driver with wood
drill bit

Wood screws

Paint and paintbrush

Pencil

Fret saw

Black Sharpie

Wood glue

Clamps or masking tape

2 D-rings

Matt outdoor varnish

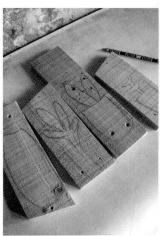

1 Cut the planks to length and the strip wood to the height of the five planks when they are laid flat and pushed together, in my case this is 15½ inches (39cm). Sand the cut edges. Screw the strip wood to the back of the planks to hold them together, 2¾ inches (7cm) from the edge and pre-drilling the holes to prevent the wood splitting. Sand the wood smooth.

2 Paint the front and edges of the wood—I used Annie Sloan Chalk Paint® in Provence. Let dry.

3 On your scrap pieces, draw vase, leaf, and flower shapes with a pencil.

4 Cut out your shapes using a fret saw and sand them smooth.

5 Paint your shapes any color you like—I used Annie Sloan Chalk Paint® in Old White, Amsterdam Green, Olive, and English Yellow. Let dry.

6 When the paint is dry, you can add detail to the cutouts using a black Sharpie.

7 Glue the pieces to the front of the painted board. Keep them in place with clamps or masking tape until the glue is dry.

8 Screw two D-rings to the wood strips on the back so you can hang your artwork. If hanging outside, give the whole piece a coat of matt outdoor varnish.

CANDLE AND TEALIGHT HOLDERS

Pallets are made from a wide variety of wood, and projects like this one really showcase the different colors and textures. Created from offcuts left over from other makes, these candlesticks and tealight holders make great handmade gifts that are very easy to construct.

YOU WILL NEED:

Pallet wood offcuts

Measuring rule

Saw

Wood glue

Clamps

Palm sander

Drill with ⅞-inch (22-mm) paddle drill piece for a candle or 1½-inch (40-mm) for a tealight

Teak oil (or other wood oil) and a lint-free cloth

1 Each holder needs four or five pieces of wood cut to the same shape. I used triangles for the candlestick and rectangles for the tealight holder. The triangles are formed from two 3¼ x 3¼-inch (8 x 8-cm) squares cut in half. The rectangles measure 3½ x 3 inches (9 x 7.5cm).

2 Spread the glue over one entire side of the offcut (I like to use a paint stirrer or spare piece of thin wood or plastic for this).

3 Stack all your pieces on top of each other, then apply clamps to make sure the pieces of wood are packed together as tightly as possible. Let dry for a day.

4 Remove the clamps and sand the wood as smooth as you can—the longer you sand, the better the results. Use a coarse paper first and finish with a finer grid one. I also used my palm sander to round off all the edges and corners.

5 Drill a ⅞-inch (22-mm) hole to fit your candle, going to a maximum depth of 1¼ inches (3cm). For a tealight, use a 1½-inch (40-mm) paddle bit and only drill ½ inch (1cm) deep.

6 Oil the wood to really bring out the grain.

STACKED VASE

I love this vase as it's so playful. It looks complicated, but is in fact very easy to make. You can make your vase as large or as small as you wish, depending on the glass bottle you use inside. I like having fresh flowers on my outdoor dining table and this pallet wood vase is great to keep outdoors all year round. This is also a great way to use up offcuts left over from other projects.

YOU WILL NEED:

Pallet wood planks

Measuring rule

Saw

Pen or pencil

Compasses

Glass bottle or jar

Fret saw or jigsaw

Drill driver with wood drill bit

Palm sander or sandpaper

Wood glue

Clamps

Paint and varnish, plus paintbrush (optional)

Matt outdoor varnish

1 Cut your pallet wood into squares or rectangles slightly larger than your bottle or jar—my pieces are 4 x 3¼ inches (10 x 8cm). You will need enough blocks of wood for the stack to be slightly taller than your bottle.

2 Find the middle on one block by drawing diagonal lines from corner to corner, then draw a circle centrally on the wood using compasses, with the point placed where the lines cross. This is the hole you will cut out for the bottle, so it needs to be quite a bit larger than the bottle to ensure it can be easily inserted.

3 Cut out the circle using a fret saw or jigsaw. First drill a hole in the center with a wood drill bit to fit the blade in, then cut out the circle. This piece will be your template for cutting all the other blocks, so check at this stage that the hole is large enough to accommodate the bottle.

4 On all but one block, trace the bottle space and cut all the holes out. Sand the blocks smooth on all sides, including the block without a hole cut into it (this forms the base of the vase).

5 Apply the wood glue to the blocks, spreading it close to the cut-out circle, and start stacking. It helps to place the bottle in the middle to make sure you stick and stack correctly. Twist the wood blocks slightly as you go higher to create the wave effect. Make sure the bottle is not accidentally glued in place as you will need to remove it for cleaning.

6 Carefully remove the bottle and clamp all the blocks in position. Leave the clamps on for as long as it states on the glue bottle (this is usually several hours).

7 When the glue has completely set, remove the clamps, then sand the vase. If you wish, you can paint it and/or apply an outdoor varnish to make it weatherproof. I painted my vase a vibrant blue using Annie Sloan Chalk Paint® in Aubusson Blue, then gave it a coat of matt outdoor varnish when dry.

VASE RACK

This rack of vases will look great in the middle of your outdoor dining table! Created from just one plank and three glass bottles from my recycling bin, it is a very quick project to make. You can use old milk bottles, used soda bottles, or three little vases if there is nothing suitable in your recycling bin. If you have a long dining table, why not use more bottles and stretch it out over the entire length of your table!

YOU WILL NEED:

Pallet wood plank

3 glass bottles, all the same height

Measuring rule

Saw

Palm sander or sandpaper

Wood glue

Nail gun or hammer and nails

Drill driver with paddle drill bit

Pencil

1 Line up the three bottles on the plank of wood to decide how long the wood needs to be—for me, this is 12½ inches (32cm). Cut two pieces to this length and sand smooth.

2 Cut two more pieces from the plank. These need to be the height of the vases plus the thickness of your wood—for me, this is 9 inches (23cm). Sand smooth. Glue and then nail the side pieces to the base plank.

3 On the top plank, decide where the openings need to be for the necks of the vases, making sure they are evenly spaced. Trace around the top of the bottle with a pencil.

4 Using a paddle drill bit with the same width (or slightly bigger, but not smaller), drill the vase openings.

5 Stand the vases in place on the base of the rack. Add the top piece, with the vase necks positioned in the drilled holes. Glue and then carefully nail the top piece to the frame.

MADE BY HAND

THE SCANDINAVIAN HOME

NOMAD   SIBELLA COURT

HOUSE OF PLANTS

SELINA LAKE   GARDEN STYLE

WOOD-CLAD WALL

Want to add texture to your shed or summerhouse? Clad your walls in timber! As well as being used for creating and building my book projects, my workshop doubles up as my photo studio and this wall makes everything I photograph look amazing. It also provides the perfect backdrop for my writing desk, and a lovely spot to catch up on emails and reading my favorite interior style books. For this project I used every single piece of spare wood I had lying around—as well as pallets, I used planks left over from other builds, reclaimed floorboards, and a few dismantled projects.

This could be an ongoing project—just add more cladding when you have wood left from other builds!

YOU WILL NEED:

Batons (see step 1)—I used three ¾ x 1½ x 94½ inches (2cm x 4cm x 2.4m), but use more if you want to clad a wider expanse of wall

Pallet wood, floorboards, leftover planks, or whatever you have lying around

Measuring rule

Drill driver with wood drill bit and masonry drill bit

Wall plugs

Hammer (optional)

Wood screws (length depends on thickness of your wood)

Saw

Palm sander or sandpaper

Small amount of black and/ or gray paint and small paintbrush

1 If you have a wooden shed, you can skip this step and screw the cladding directly into the wooden walls/posts. If you have a brick building, you have to put up batons to attach the wooden planks to. I wanted to use up all my spare pieces of wood so put a baton every 12 inches (30cm) to allow me to use shorter pieces of wood. If you just use 39-inch (100-cm) planks, you can put batons up every 31 inches (80cm).

2 Decide where you want to place the upright batons, then drill holes in your wall using a masonry drill bit and push or hammer a wall plug into each hole.

3 Line your baton up against the wall, mark the position of the wall plugs, and drill holes in the wood using the wood drill bit.

4 Screw the baton to the wall. Repeat with the remaining batons.

5 Starting at the bottom of the wall, begin screwing the wood to the batons.

6 Add subsequent levels of wood, fitting the pieces together like a jigsaw and making sure you mix different colors and textures. If any planks are too long, saw them to size to create a neat edge.

7 If you need longer pieces of timber to fit in between the batons, you can add a small piece of wood on the reverse side to join them together.

8 Continue in this way until your whole wall is clad in wood.

9 Sand the edges and surface of the wood smooth—it's best to use a palm sander for this as it will be quicker and you will get a smoother result.

10 To hide the screw heads, paint them with a small dab of dark paint.

WHITEWASHED LANTERN

Nothing adds atmosphere to your outdoor space as quickly and easily as a couple of lanterns. Whether you use a solar light or a jam jar with a candle inside, they will make long summer evenings or impromptu winter alfresco lunches a cozy affair. I made mine from very rough pallet wood planks to give the lanterns a rustic feel. Pallet wood comes in all conditions and sometimes the very rough, almost broken planks work well in projects like this.

YOU WILL NEED:

Solar light or jam jar and candle/tealight

Pallet wood planks

Batten—I used 1¼ x ½ inch (32 x 10mm), but a smaller size works too

Measuring rule

Pencil

Saw

Palm sander or sandpaper

Wood glue

Nail gun or hammer and nails

White paint and paintbrush

Drill driver with wood drill bit

³/₈-inch (8-mm) sisal rope, 20 inches (50cm) long

Sturdy needle, thimble, and strong thread

I MADE TWO LANTERNS OF DIFFERENT HEIGHTS. THE TALLER ONE HAS SIDES THAT ARE 12 INCHES (30CM) HIGH, WHILE THE SMALLER ONE HAS SIDES OF 7½ INCHES (19CM). THEIR BASES ARE THE SAME SIZE.

1 To make the base of the lantern, place your solar light or jam jar on a wide piece of pallet wood or scrap piece of wood and mark where you need to cut the timber. There should be enough space around the light for it to be lifted in and out. My base measures 4¾ x 4¾ inches (12 x 12cm). Cut and sand the wood.

2 From the batten, make a square frame the same size as the base. For me, that is two pieces 4¾ inches (12cm) long and two pieces 4 inches (10cm) long. Glue and then nail them together to form a square frame.

3 To make the side slats of the lantern, cut five 7½-inch (19-cm) lengths of pallet plank, then cut each piece in half widthwise. Sand the pieces smooth.

4 Paint all the wood (base, frame, and side slats) white and let dry. If the lantern is to be left outside, use paint suitable for outdoor use. I painted my lantern quite roughly for a whitewashed effect.

5 Now attach the side slats to the square frame (this will be the top of the lantern). Glue and nail the slats to the frame, extending them ½ inch (1cm) above the frame. Space the slats equidistantly—the front and back of the lantern have three slats, extending beyond the frame by the thickness of the wood.

6 The sides have two slats which slot in between the extended slats, butting up to them.

7 Position the base 1¼ inches (3cm) up from the bottom of the slats, and glue and nail in place.

8 For the rope handle, drill a hole into the square frame between the two slats.

9 Push the rope through the holes, fold it back on itself, and stitch together firmly. Repeat on the other side. You may need to use a thimble to push the needle through the rope. You will also need to use a sturdy needle which won't break.

10 As a finishing touch, wrap the thread around the joins and stitch to secure in place. Pop the light inside.

INDEX

RESOURCES

- You can find pallets at your local lumber yard, DIY center, or on building sites (also see page 8).

In the UK:
Travis Perkins (travisperkins.co.uk), B&Q (diy.com)

In the US:
Home depot (homedepot.com), Lowe's (lowes.com)

- Also have a look on local Facebook groups, Freecycle, and Gumtree (facebook.com, freecycle.org, gumtree.com)

- You can purchase pallets already dismantled, cleaned, and sanded from The Little Lodge (thelittlelodge.co.uk)

- All fabric in book is from Cloth & Candy (clothandcandy.com) who stock the loveliest printed cottons.

- Find beautiful tiles in the Porcelain Superstore (delivery worldwide, porcelainsuperstore.co.uk). The tiles in the mosaic table are by Topps Tiles (toppstiles.co.uk).

- All power tools used in the book are by Ryobi—I really like their cordless One+ range (uk.ryobitools.eu andryobitools.com)

- I use a lot of Annie Sloan Chalk Paints®. To make them suitable for outdoor use with a waterproof varnish (anniesloan.com).

- Ikea is great for table legs—I used theirs on the mosaic table and the pallet sofas (ikea.com). Legs on the chevron table are by the Hairpin Leg Company (thehairpinlegcompany.co.uk).

- Artificial flowers by Hobbycraft (hobbycraft.co.uk), for USA try Michaels (michaels.com). Ikea has a great selection too (ikea.com).

- All glue used is by Gorilla (gorillaglue.com). I think they have the best wood glue.

- I like Wilko (wilko.com) for everything you might need from the dog bed pillow to cushions and small building materials. In the USA try Target (target.com).

- The metal hanging planters on the slatted fence are by Ikea (ikea.com).

- All plants are from my florist, local garden center, and MarMar Margate (ramsgateflorist.co.uk, wyevalegardencentres.co.uk, instagram.com/marmarmargate).

- I love using the vinyl backdrops from Capture by Lucy for my step-by-step photos (capturebylucy.com/backdrops).

Shot on location at Hester's house, Clare Youngs' house (clareyoungs.co.uk), Edward and Tina Woollard's house (homefarmlocation.com), Sophie Burch's house (instagram.com/mammaburch), and Nick Hanna's retreat (highwealdretreatcentre.com).

I get a lot of building inspiration from magazines, blogs, and Instagram. Here are some of my favorites:

Cereal magazine (readcereal.com)—stunning photography and travel inspiration.

Kinfolk (kinfolk.com)—for beautiful layouts and inspiring interiors.

VT Wonen (vtwonen.nl)—Dutch interior and DIY magazine which gives you a great look at the toned-down but fun design the Dutch do so well.

Martha Stewart Magazine (marthastewart.com)—the queen bee of everything craft, this magazine needs to be on everybody's reading list.

The Magnolia Journal (magnolia.com/journal)—I love everything Chip and Joanna do!

Conde Nast Traveller (cntraveller.com)—a travel magazine, but their images are immensely inspiring.

abeautifulmess.com—Elsie and Emma have such a fresh and unique approach to home decor and craft.

fallfordiy.com—I love all of Fran's makes and builds.

grillo-designs.com—Medina does great things in her rental home, go check it out.

blog.westelm.com—the Front + Main blog from interior mastermind West Elm.

studiodiy.com—I'm a big fan of Kelly's Instagram feed and stories.

sweetpaulmag.com—the magazine, blog, and Instagram are all great—everything Paul Lowe touches is magic.

ACKNOWLEDGMENTS

Thank you to everyone at Cico Books for trusting me with another book, especially Cindy, Penny, Sally, and Anna. To Pete and Gillian for their amazing editing and for making my scribbles look half decent. To Geoff for the great design of this book, and the always brilliant James Gardiner for capturing the builds so beautifully.

A massive thank you to Ann and Mike for all their hard work in making my garden look photoshoot-ready—maybe one day I will finally turn into a gardener :)

Thanks go to Clare, Sophie, Edward and Tina, and Nick for letting me shoot in their gardens.

I have to give a shout out to Ian as he never complains when I fill our garden with a mountain of pallets waiting to be turned into projects—thank you. And of course, to my parents, who worked their magic when I was little and ignited the DIY bug in me.

FOR MORE INFORMATION ON HESTER

www.hestershandmadehome.com
www.youtube.com/handmadehome
www.instagram.com/byhestergrams
www.twitter.com/hestershandmade
www.facebook.com/hestershandmadehome